Contributing Authors
Brad McBride
Julie Souder, M. Ed.
Debbie West

Editor
Jeri Wilcox

Editorial Project Manager
Ina Massler Levin, M.A.

Editor-in-Chief
Sharon Coan, M.S. Ed.

Illustrator
Howard Chaney

Art Director
Elayne Roberts

Cover Artist
Sue Fullam

Imaging
Alfred Lau
Ralph Olmedo, Jr.
James Edward Grace

Product Manager
Phil Garcia

Publishers
Rachelle Cracchiolo, M.S. Ed.
Mary Dupuy Smith, M.S. Ed.

How to Manage Your Multi-Age Classroom

Grades 3–5

Author

Angela Bean Bolton, M.S.

Teacher Created Materials, Inc.
6421 Industry Way
Westminster, CA 92683
www.teachercreated.com

Reprinted, 2000
Made in U.S.A.
ISBN-1-55734-328-4

Table of Contents

Table of Contents *(cont.)*

Introduction

This book is a valuable resource for teachers, containing explanations, suggestions, descriptions, and learning activities for those who are interested in providing a program that offers continuous progress for every child.

A Compact Overview of Contents:

- an explanation of the rationale of Multi-Age grouping
- an explanation of the advantages and disadvantages of Multi-Age grouping
- encouragement for those in transition to a Multi-Age program
- a description of the characteristics of a Multi-Age classroom
- suggestions for practical application of Multi-Age ideas
- tips for organizing curriculum and grouping students
- sample learning center activities
- suggestions for creating an appropriate classroom atmosphere for Multi-Age grouping
- tips for encouraging parental involvement
- answers to questions often asked by teachers about Multi-Age grouping

This handbook is based on a classroom teacher's understanding, training, and experiences as she made the transition from a traditional fourth grade teacher to a 3rd, 4th, and 5th grade Multi-Age teacher. Many of the ideas in this book are the result of the collaborated efforts of all team members and school staff.

Introducing
the
Multi-Age
Classroom

Multi-Age Definitions

3rd

4th

5th

BSA—Beginning School Activity—A brief task for students to work on when they enter the classroom every morning. It may involve a review or application of skills previously taught or provide practice of basic skills.

Block Scheduling—Time allotted for specific activities.

Centers—Learning activities available throughout the classroom.

Continuous Progress—Planning for and providing on-going individual achievement.

Flexible grouping—Arranging students in order to provide optimal learning situations for the greatest number of children possible.

ISA—Integrated Subject Activities including social studies, science, art, physical education, and technology activities relating to the theme.

Ladder math—A series of math computation problems, including addition, subtraction, multiplication, and division, listed on a page in order of increasing difficulty, used approximately twice a month to assess each child's computational progress.

Literature-based—A method of curriculum planning that integrates a variety of subject areas with selected pieces of literature.

Needs Grouping—Grouping students during a scheduled block of time, such as math or writing, in order to meet specific needs.

Pod—Group of 2–4 classes which function cooperatively, rotating among their homerooms for block scheduling, needs grouping, centers, and whole group activities.

Three-Year Cycle—A curriculum framework where subject areas and topics are arranged yearly by a common theme and by selected children's literature in three-year rotation.

Spiraling Topics—Revisiting topics periodically to address and provide increased understanding.

Web—a concise outline of related curriculum topics that provides a framework for organizing units of study.

Webbing—The process of listing curriculum areas that are related to a particular theme or pieces of literature.

Rationale for Multi-Age Grouping

What happens in schools affects individuals and communities. With so much riding on public education, everyone must take part in educational innovations. Students, parents, community representatives, teachers, and administrators are encouraged to find, implement, and support beneficial strategies that increase student learning, progress, and achievement. Multi-Age programs offer one promising solution.

The Need for the Multi-Age Classroom

In the 1840's, Horace Mann implemented the first graded classrooms in the United States. The structure of the school was bound by 180-day increments, and children began school in kindergarten at age five. The steps for students to climb were established by adults who needed to account for and manage children. Student readiness did not have a significant impact on the system.

Multi-Age educators have recognized that children are individuals with different needs, backgrounds, learning styles, and personalities. They feel it is time to organize the structure of schools in order to provide opportunities for all children to grow and develop at their individual rates. They perceive a natural learning environment that calls for heterogeneous, Multi-Age groupings, within which other groupings may be created as needed.

Multi-Age groups usually include two or three consecutive grades with three to four age levels. This age range is necessary because children enter kindergarten at diverse developmental stages. An increase in the number of low birth weight babies, poverty, and divorce, as well as other changing demographics of our society, contribute to this diversity. Multi-Age settings more readily accommodate learning variables, allowing students who are ready to proceed, an opportunity for rapid acceleration, while others who need more time are able to develop at their individual rates.

Emphasis Is Focused on Individual Rate of Progress

Since Multi-Age does not emphasize or spotlight a child's grade level, it can be contrasted to split-grade programs where students of usually two ages are combined but taught separately in the same classroom at their traditional grade levels. Split-grade programs, which are often created to manage class size issues, do not have a core Multi-Age belief, are usually not multi-year classes, and do not focus on continuous progress. A continuous progress curriculum allows children to move on as rapidly as they master content or to repeat content in different ways to gain better understanding.

What Is Multi-Age?

Multi-Age Programs Are . . .	Multi-Age Programs Are Not . . .
• developmentally appropriate strategies.	• "lock-step" systems with little regard for student interests.
• heterogeneous communities of learners.	• based on rigid groupings.
• supportive of continuous learning.	• time-based know and recall.
• based on emotional, social, intellectual, and physical growth.	• based solely on intellectual learning.
• providing integrated learning activities.	• isolated learning of subjects and tests.
• promoting active student involvement.	• forcing students to "bear with it."
• using a wide range of materials.	• primarily paper and pencil tasks.
• implementing authentic assessments.	• drill and test method of education.
• involving teachers as co-learners and facilitators.	• directed by a teacher as an authoritarian and know-it-all.
• child-centered.	• teacher centered.
• promoting teamwork and diversity.	• designed to promote isolation and conformation.
• renewing energy and support for education.	• producing students who become burned out and frustrated with education.
• supportive and nurturing environments.	• environments with fear of failure.

Advantages and Disadvantages of Multi-Age Groupings

The advantages of a Multi-Age classroom

- Students experience the security and stability of having the same teacher for several years.
- A close relationship develops between the child, child's family, and the teacher.
- Knowing he will have the child in class the next year, a Multi-Age teacher's commitment to and understanding of each child's learning and progress grows.
- Teachers focus on the child's whole development: physical, intellectual, social, and emotional.
- There is more flexibility for students because attention is given to individual needs.
- Children learn the routine, and teachers can pick up where they left off.
- The child belongs to a learning community and develops a positive attitude about school.
- It expands the age range of peers, unites students, and promotes cooperative learning.
- It allows for student diversity and fosters acceptance.
- There are varied opportunities for leadership for all ages along with additional exposure to challenging activities.
- It encourages socialization, independence, and interaction with peers.
- It favors more authentic practical assessments.

The disadvantages of a Multi-Age classroom

- It may be too overwhelming for some children, parents, and teachers.
- Teachers neglect to challenge advanced children and take advantage of them as tutors.
- The classroom population is too diverse.
- More time is spent with the neediest children.
- Children may need more one-on-one attention; some children may feel neglected.
- Some students are easily distracted.
- Children may compare themselves negatively, feeling they can't do something as well as others.
- Personality clashes may develop.
- Teachers have a lot of work, planning instruction for a wide range of student abilities.
- Teachers may have unrealistic expectations for themselves and become frustrated.

Questions and Answers Often Asked About Multi-Age Grouping

How is Multi-Age different from traditional single grade programs?

Multi-Age grouping is the purposeful and intentional grouping of children of more than one age and ability level together to find the greatest benefit of interaction among them. Multi-Age programs expect children to have different interests, abilities, and skills. All children in Multi-Age programs learn at their own pace within a supportive, challenging environment that encourages growth and development without fear of failure.

How do you decide what you are going to teach and when? Will the curriculum be covered?

Multi-Age teachers work together as a team to group curriculum objectives into integrated thematic units that can be taught over the course of the Multi-Age program, usually two to three years. There is a focus on Language Arts and Mathematics objectives throughout the three-year cycle, while social studies and science objectives may be designated for a particular year in the cycle. Individual student progress is constantly monitored.

How do you grade or assess students in a Multi-Age classroom?

Multi-Age educators do not rely primarily on paper and pencil tests to evaluate student performance. They typically use standardized test results as one indicator of instructional needs and abilities. Authentic assessment strategies that call for students to solve life-related problems and prepare portfolios of their work spring naturally from Multi-Age instructional strategies. Also, teachers often keep anecdotal records and checklists of skills to monitor individual progress.

Based upon your experience, do you think lower skilled children make more progress in a Multi-Age class compared to their progress in a single graded class?

Even though Multi-Age teachers expect and intentionally plan for children with fewer abilities, Multi-Age should not be a "dumping ground" for those students. Lower skilled children can make outstanding improvements if they are willing to participate appropriately in learning activities, desire to learn school material, and have a supportive and dedicated home environment. Multi-Age relieves the pressure of failure while setting high standards for students. Lower ability children also respond well to flexible grouping.

Based upon your experience, do you think average skilled children make more progress in a Multi-Age class compared to their progress in a single graded class?

Average ability students progress as well or better in a Multi-Age setting than in a traditional single grade setting. Since the Multi-Age curriculum is condensed into a three-year cycle, there is more established time for progress. In addition to continuous progress throughout the three years, Multi-Age programs provide a unique opportunity for the parents, teachers, and students to work together.

Questions and Answers *(cont.)*

Based upon your experiences, do you think above average children academically make more progress in a Multi-Age class compared to their progress in a single graded class?

Above average children are given challenging learning opportunities in a Multi-Age classroom. Goal setting conferences and independent study options provide a structure for creating challenging learning opportunities. Efforts must be made by teachers, parents, and students to continuously outline academic progress standards for the accelerated student. Students also serve as peer tutors. Multi-Age looks not only at academic achievement, but also at a child's social, emotional, and physical growth. Flexible grouping options benefit all ability levels.

Should Multi-Age classrooms include special needs students?

It can be frustrating for a classroom teacher in severe situations where a special needs student prevents or denies the learning of others. Nevertheless, almost all children have individual or "special" needs at some time due to family circumstances, health, personal feelings, or disabilities. Multi-Age offers a variety of learning experiences and opportunities to make accommodations for student diversity. Many Multi-Age programs include resource personnel as team members who provide support as recommended.

Does current research support the concept of Multi-Age?

Current knowledge explains that learners construct their own knowledge by connecting what they are trying to learn to their previous experiences and understanding. When implemented correctly, Multi-Age programs reflect the current assumptions and research about environments conducive to learning. Multi-Age environments provide active hands-on experiences, integrated concepts, goal setting, daily written and oral communications, individualization, cooperative learning, explorations, self assessments, and conferencing.

How are Multi-Age programs organized?

There is a variety of Multi-Age grouping configurations. Grades K–2, 1–3, K–3, 1–2, 3–5, 4–5, and 3–6 illustrate a few of the organizations.

How does Multi-Age grouping affect teachers?

Teaching a Multi-Age class takes more planning initially, but many teachers who have been implementing hands-on-learning, whole language strategies, curriculum integration, literature based instruction, and writing across the curriculum find that it is not that different from teaching a single grade class. There is also the benefit of already knowing many of the students, how they learn, what they are able to do, and how to interact with their parents for several successive years. Teachers need to be familiar with curriculum objectives for multiple grade levels. Also, they need to be organized yet flexible enough to try new things.

What suggestions can you give us as we start a Multi-Age program?

Take "baby steps" and go slowly. Allow teachers who personally enjoy learning to volunteer to work together on a Multi-Age team. Then provide teachers with initial, as well as ongoing, training. Work with the total school faculty to have others consider their roles in a Multi-Age setting, encouraging cooperation rather than competition among staff members. Administrative interest and support is necessary for program success. Similarily, principals must be actively involved as positive facilitators of teacher decision-making.

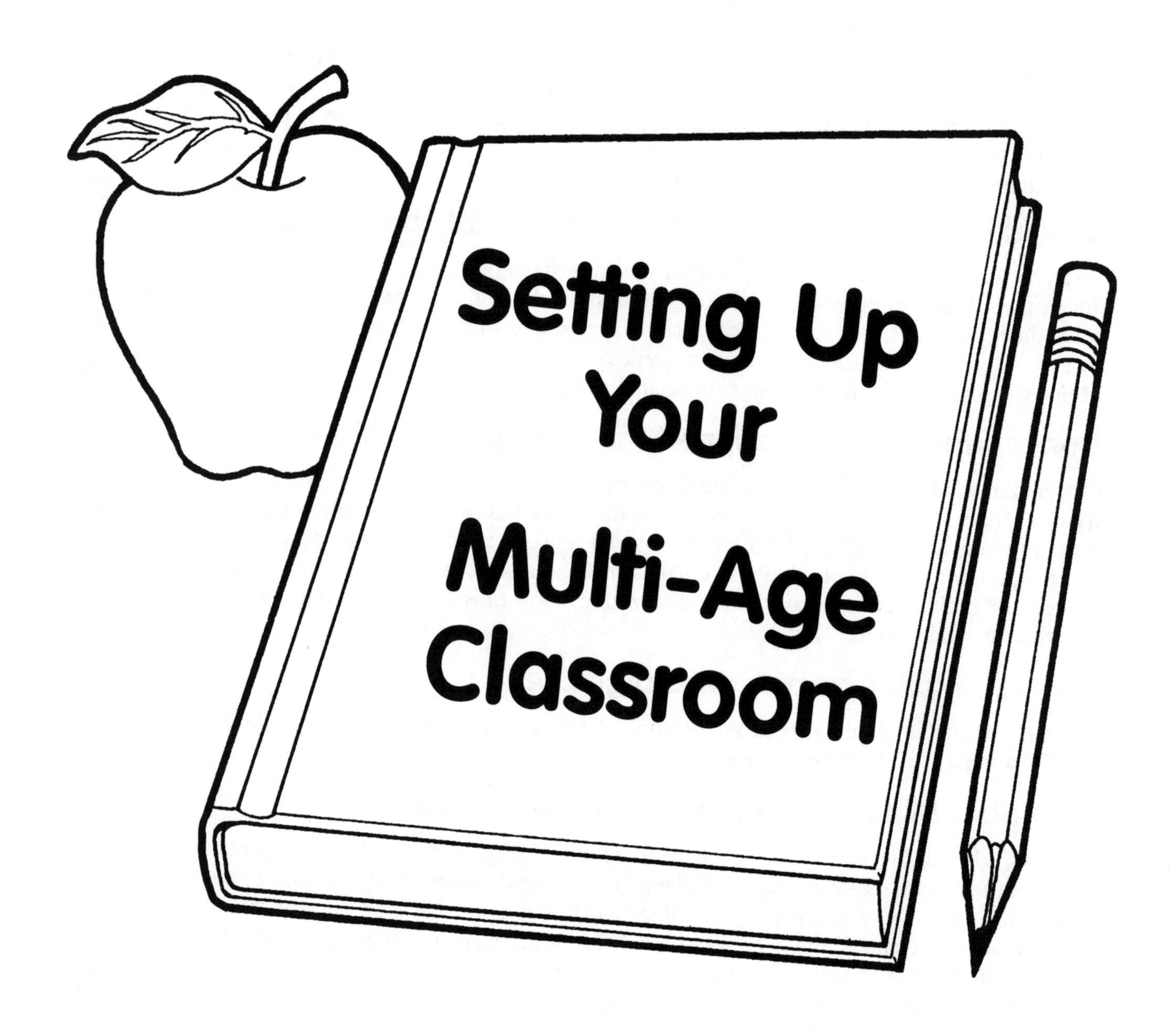
Setting Up
Your
Multi-Age
Classroom

Implementation

Almost every time a new program is implemented, there is a time of feeling unsure or uncomfortable with the changing process. Nevertheless, by taking what can be used and applying that toward making beneficial changes, the end result can come out better than before. To avoid feeling overwhelmed, set one to three goals for your classroom each month. Remember to celebrate accomplishing the goals. It helps to look at your teaching as a learning process as well. You may continue to make changes in your classroom and procedures each year. Also, let others know when you need more support and encouragement.

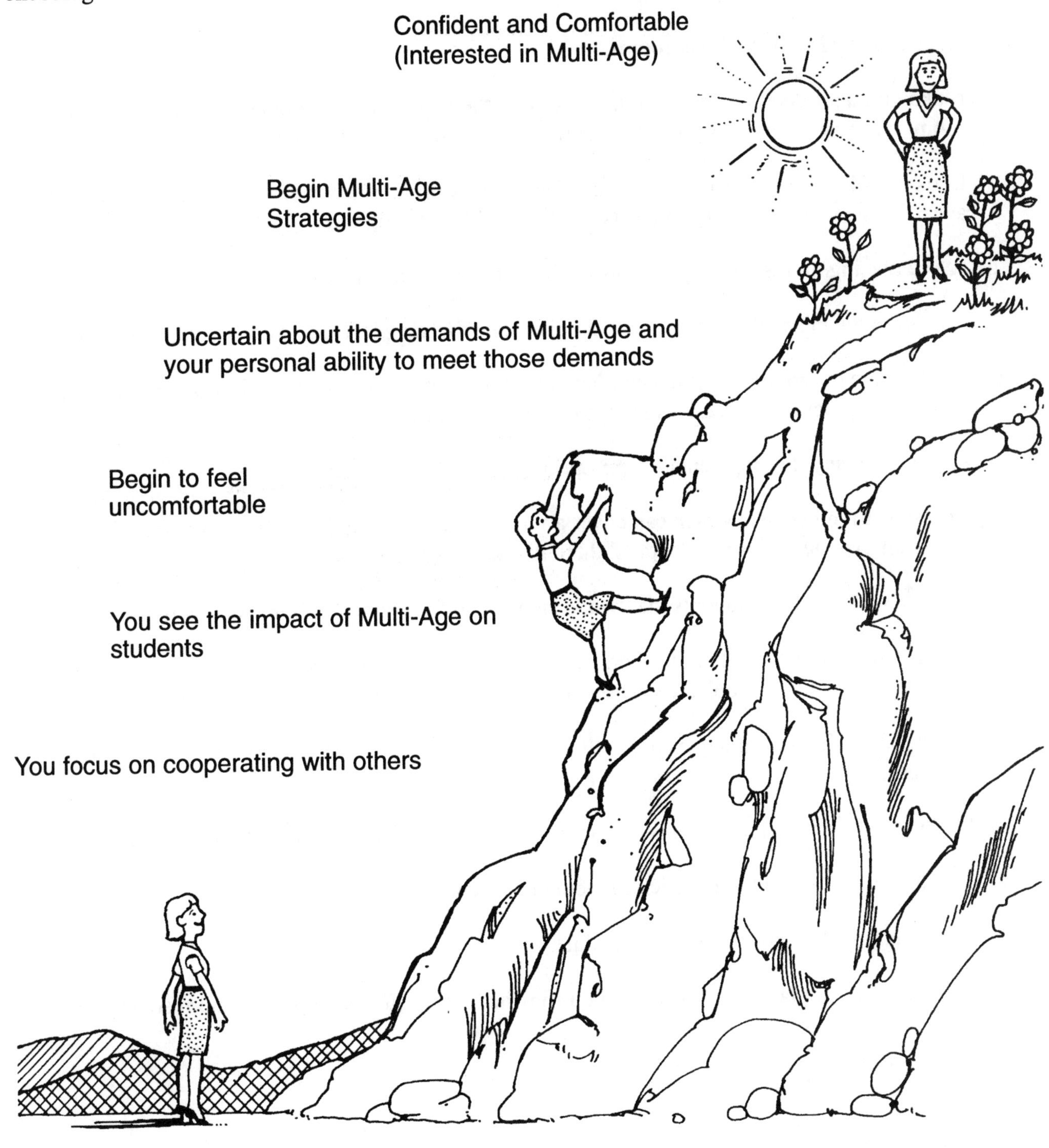

Points of Interest

These suggestions can help you prepare for teaching a Multi-Age classroom.

1. Once you have administrative support, find other teachers (a partner or team) with a similar philosophy and commitment with whom you can work well.
2. Read articles about Multi-Age information and research. Discuss and determine your fundamental beliefs and goals.
3. Visit existing Multi-Age classrooms.
4. Make all major decisions as a team: scheduling the day, choosing thematic units, arranging the room, purchasing supplies, and other duties. Delegate responsibilities evenly.
5. Look closely at the heterogeneous mix of each classroom. Each room should contain a mixture of ages, genders, ability levels, interests, social needs, and ethnicities.
6. Avoid placing all discipline problems or lower level children in the same classroom.
7. Condense the curriculum into a realistic plan (See the sample Three-Year Cycle, page 23).
8. Concentrate on grouping mandated objectives for science and social studies together for yearly themes, and focus on objectives for the older children first.
9. Collect as many developmentally appropriate materials as you can.
10. Design learning centers which can cover a wide range of ability levels, including problem-solving, hands-on experiences, and integrated thematic activities.
11. Provide spaces where students may work independently and spaces for group activities.
12. Design opportunities so that members on your team may have a significant amount of shared planning time. For example, ask that your team's special classes be scheduled at the same time.
13. Decide on evaluation strategies that will provide authentic, diagnostic information for you and parents.
14. Identify tasks with which parents can help, and recruit as many volunteers as you can.
15. Set clear classroom rules and stick to them consistently as a team.
16. Plan intentionally and stick to the schedule.
17. Have designated places for finished and unfinished work, student supplies, and resource materials.

Teaming

Although a Multi-Age program can function effectively in one classroom, being part of a team with common purpose and goals can help to make a Multi-Age program even more successful. The team typically is composed of two to four teachers who combine their students and classrooms to become the pod unit. Within the pod, students report to their homeroom at the beginning of each day, then are rotated through other participating rooms for block scheduling, needs grouping, centers, and individual attention.

Each member on the team can have a significant role and contribute toward accomplishing the group's purpose. Team members can work together and cooperate to get things done more quickly and easily than by working alone. They may also solve problems and make decisions together, so no one has to feel alone and solely responsible. Team members can count on each other; they are able to give each other mutual support. They can work with each other to evaluate and improve their team's performance. Furthermore, it is important for team members to communicate among themselves, even when things are not going well. Holding regularly scheduled meetings which include the principal and other appropriate staff members is an excellent opportunity for free exchange of observations and ideas to help further the goals of the Multi-Age program.

Check with your local university to see if they have an Intern Program or Student Teacher program for additional participants who can actively contribute to the team.

Teacher jobs that can be split up among team members:

- Scheduling field trips
- Television and newspaper publicity
- Community relations
- Technology training and instruction
- Centers
- Remediation activities
- Scheduling aides and volunteers
- Taking care of pod area pets
- Morning announcements
- Bulletin boards
- Printing charts
- Leading songs
- Leading exercise
- Designing authentic assessments
- Collecting library resources
- Preparing notes to parents
- Multi-Age team leader
- Ordering and purchasing materials
- Video and filmstrip set-up
- Scheduling, inviting, and acknowledging guest speakers
- Staff committees (equally distributed)

Placement Procedure

Assigning children to individual teachers takes into account several factors to make sure that each class is organized in the best way. Multi-Age teams generally work together to make recommendations with respect to the placement of each child. In fact, primary teachers often collaborate with middle grade Multi-Age teachers to determine appropriate student placement. Also, parents may be encouraged to visit the classrooms and communicate their own concerns and preferences. Teachers may ask that parents tell them what kinds of things have worked well for their children in the past, the children's strengths and weaknesses, and what they would want their children to work toward during the next year.

The following criteria are important to consider regarding placement:

- The child's educational needs
- Academic ability—independent, accelerated, average, struggling
- The child's social, emotional, and physical needs
- Parental input
- Distribution of special needs children among teachers
- Approximate equal number of children in each class
- Balanced representation of cultures in each class

Heterogeneous grouping is encouraged. Each room should contain a mixture of ages, ability levels, and social needs. Flexible grouping is used, including the integration of special education students.

The following categories may be helpful in distinguishing between student personalities. You may want to add more descriptors of your own.

Academic

- accelerated
- achiever
- average
- bilingual
- creative
- disorganized
- learning disabled
- off-task
- struggling
- special needs
- unmotivated
- verbal

Social

- assertive
- challenger
- competitive
- follower
- interrupts
- manipulative
- perfectionist
- shy
- street-wise
- talkative
- tattles
- uncooperative

Emotional

- alarmist
- clingy
- confident
- dependent
- exaggerates
- imaginative
- immature
- independent
- rebellious
- risk-taker
- stubborn
- whiner

Physical

- aggressive
- athletic
- handicapped
- hyperactive
- impulsive
- lazy
- restless; fidgety
- uncoordinated

Adapted from Mary Garmella, *SDE's Multi-Age Classrooms: The Ungrading of America's Schools*, 1993.

Child Placement Form for Parents

Dear Parents,

We, the staff of ________________________________ are planning for the __________ school year and need your input. Listed below are possible educational choices which will be offered to our students. Please indicate which choices might best fit the needs of your child. Openings in some programs are limited and may have waiting lists. Below is listed a comparison of the two program choices:

Regular Graded Program	**Multi-Age Program**
Students of the same grade are in classes together.	Students of several ages are in classes together.
Student has a different teacher each year.	Student remains with the same team of teachers over several years and is provided the opportunity for continuous progress in learning as well as in teacher/student relations.
Student has different classmates each year.	Student stays with the same group of students. Changes occur as older students exit the class and younger students join the class.
Cooperative learning takes place among same age peers.	Cooperative learning takes place between older and younger students on a continuous basis.
Thematic teaching uses themes that are appropriate to that grade level.	Thematic teaching uses theme cycles over a period of several years.
Student works on his or her level.	Student is given time to develop and learn over several years at an individual rate of progress.

A whole language approach to reading, integrated thematic instruction, hands-on math instruction, and individualized instruction will continue to be utilized in the elementary school program. It is our desire to continue to provide the best possible educational program for your child. If you have any questions or concerns please let us know.

Sincerely,

____

Principal

- -

My child ____________________________ is in __________ this year.
(grade/class)

The choice for my child is:

______ a program with regular grades (Kindergarten, 1st, 2nd, 3rd, 4th, and 5th)

______ a Multi-Age program (Multi-Age groups of primary or intermediate age students)

______ No preference

This form should be returned by ____________________. If the form is not returned, we will assume that you have no preferences as to your child's placement.

Parent Signature ____________________________

Family Involvement

Family involvement is a critical component of a student's success in a Multi-Age program. Parents seem to be more supportive of Multi-Age when they feel ownership in the decision of placing their children in a Multi-Age setting. Parents are expected to be active participants in the education of their children and are encouraged to volunteer in the classroom. Some parents may even volunteer to complete tasks at home or support the class financially by providing needed classroom supplies.

The teaching team should decide each year the tasks that parents could help with. Family members can assist teachers by giving individual spelling tests, reviewing math facts with children, recording trade books, making charts, filling out book orders, reading, and discussing learning with children. In fact, training a parent for a particular task and scheduling a consistent time for him or her to be in the classroom has proven to be most beneficial. Furthermore, sending home a survey may give parents direction as to ways in which they can provide a service to the classroom.

Name tags can be provided for parents to wear while they are volunteering at the school to help promote a sense of appreciation and recognition.

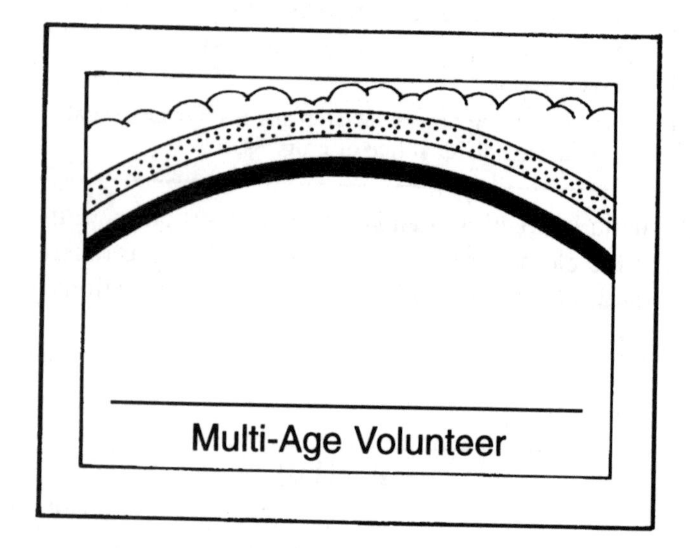

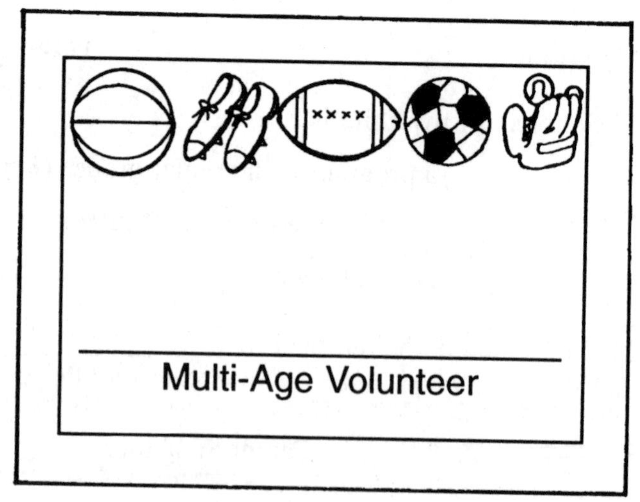

Multi-Age Volunteer Survey Form

Dear Parents,

If you are interested in helping in the classroom in any way, please fill out this checklist and return it to school. Put a check by the activities in which you would like to participate. We are planning an after school training session so you will understand just how you can help! When working with the children, we cannot promise that you will be with your own child. Many of the things we will have you make or do will benefit all Multi-Age classes.

Name: ______________________________

Child ______________________________

_______ 1. Book order preparation
_______ 2. Making charts
_______ 3. Recording trade books
_______ 4. Planning parties
_______ 5. Helping children with centers
_______ 6. Editing children's writing
_______ 7. Reading with students
_______ 8. Giving individual spelling tests
_______ 9. Field trip organizer/helper
_______ 10. Making books with students
_______ 11. Art group leader
_______ 12. Sharing a song, aerobics, or movement
_______ 13. Computer supporter
_______ 14. Photo album helper
_______ 15. Sewing books together
_______ 16. Sharing an area of expertise ______________________
_______ 17. Grading homework folders
_______ 18. Scheduling conference times
_______ 19. Reviewing math facts with students
_______ 20. Portfolio observer for another child
_______ 21. Guest speaker—related to your career
_______ 22. Teaching a foreign language
_______ 23. Other ______________________________________

Thank you for your time and help. We sincerely encourage you to come in and help with the children. We understand that it is not possible for everyone to participate in the classroom setting; however, your home encouragement and support are equally important.

Sincerely,

____

Beginning-of-the-Year Student Supplies List

Dear Parents,

Welcome to Multi-Age! We are looking forward to building and continuing some wonderful relationships, as well as growing and learning together. We encourage an open door policy and welcome your visits and questions.

If your child has previously been a member of Multi-Age, he does not need to bring items from the New Student Needs List. All students need the materials listed in the "Everyone Bring New" column. Most of the materials will be maintained by the teacher and used on appropriate assignments. Please label all supplies with your child's name.

Supplies Needed

Everyone Bring New

5 (2-inch) Metal Rings

2 #2 Pencils

Loose leaf notebook paper
(Wide-ruled, at least 200 sheets)

3 Three-ring, pocket folders

Crayons (at least 24 count)

Magic markers

2 permanent markers

Index Cards (any size)

Glue stick

2 DS/HD Computer disks

New Student Needs List

1 bound Composition book

1 Clipboard

1 Calculator

1 Ruler (inches and metric)

Scissors

Protractor (no compasses please)

2 Spiral notebooks

1 VHS Video cassette tape

Colored pencils (optional)

Tape measure (cloth or plastic)

1 Audio cassette tape

PLEASE LABEL ALL SUPPLIES!

Sincerely,

____

Recommended Classroom Materials Checklist

The following materials are recommended for each Multi-Age classroom teacher to have within easy access. Some items may be centrally located for teachers to share, while other items may be needed in individual classrooms. Also, an apple tree bulletin board entitled "Pick an Item to Donate" may be on display in the classroom at the beginning of the year. Each item needed is listed on an apple so that parents can actually "pick" an item to donate to the classroom.

For Each Child:

____ checkbook register
____ clipboard
____ composition books
____ computer disks
____ folders, pocket and prongs
____ paper, notebook
____ pencils, #2
____ pens, red and black
____ portfolio storage place
____ rings, metal 2" (5 cm)
____ video tapes, blank

Individual Classes

____ atlases
____ beans and cups
____ books, literature
____ calculators
____ calendars
____ cassette players w/ headphones
____ cassette tapes
____ clay
____ clocks
____ clothespins
____ colored pencils
____ computers
____ crayons
____ dice, blank
____ dice, official
____ dictionaries
____ facial tissue
____ flash cards, multiplication and division
____ fraction bars
____ games such as chess and checkers
____ geoboards
____ glue and glue sticks
____ index cards
____ magnets
____ maps, graphic learning
____ markers, colored art
____ markers, overhead
____ markers, transparent
____ masking tape
____ measuring tapes
____ menus, restaurant
____ overhead projector and screen
____ pattern blocks
____ pencils, colored
____ plastic storage bags
____ protractors
____ rubber bands
____ rulers
____ scissors
____ sentence strip chart
____ staplers
____ tacks
____ tangram sets
____ television
____ thesauri
____ tiles, numbered 0–9
____ unifix cubes
____ video tapes

Centrally Located

____ aluminum foil
____ aquarium
____ bags, lunch
____ balloons
____ bandages, adhesive
____ batteries
____ blender
____ books, informational
____ books, poetry
____ books, text
____ bulbs
____ camera
____ cardboard
____ chalk, colored
____ clothes hangers
____ electrical wire
____ encyclopedias
____ envelopes
____ felt
____ film projector
____ flannel boards
____ flour
____ globes
____ hot plate
____ iron
____ laserdisc player
____ magazines
____ measuring cups and spoons
____ mixer
____ mixing bowls
____ napkins
____ needles, thread
____ newspapers
____ paint
____ paintbrushes
____ paper, chart, ruled
____ paper, colored tissue
____ paper, construction
____ paper, graph
____ paper plates and cups
____ pets, classroom and supplies
____ posterboard
____ pot holders
____ pots and pans
____ rock collection
____ rubbing alcohol
____ safety glasses
____ salt
____ sandpaper
____ scale
____ screen, large
____ shells
____ soap
____ socks
____ spoons and spatulas
____ starch, liquid
____ stamps
____ thermometers
____ toaster oven
____ transparencies
____ VCR
____ video camera
____ video editor
____ vinegar
____ wallpaper and paste mix
____ wax
____ waxed paper
____ yarn

Multi-Age
Curriculum

Sample Three-Year Cycle

This chart provides an example of how to condense the curriculum into a realistic plan (A Three-Year Cycle). You may begin planning your own curriculum by reproducing a copy of your state's mandated objectives for science and social studies for third, fourth, and fifth grades. Then, group the objectives that are related to selected literature to comprise your yearly themes. Some topics may be appropriate as a minor focus each year.

Year One	Year Two	Year Three
Machines	Magnetism/Electricity	Astronomy
Friction	Sound, Heat, and Light	Plants
Habitats	Atoms and Molecular Structure	World War I and World War II
Oceanography	Weather/Climate	Culture
Geology	Three States of Matter	Immigration
Natural Resources	Forms of Energy	Map Skills*
American History	Our State's History	Change*
Revolutionary War	Regional United States	Current Events/Economy*
Westward Expansion	* Map Skills	Human Body*
Civil War	Change	Feelings/Human Behavior*
Laws/Government	* Current Events/ Economy	Nutrition/Health*
Map Skills*	*Human Body	
Historical Events:* Cause/Effect	*Feelings/Human Behavior	
Current Events/Economy*	*Nutrition/Health	
Human Body*		
Feelings/Human Behavior*		
Nutrition/Health*		

*Taught as a minor focus

Recommended Books

The following books were chosen from recommended reading selections for grades 3–5 and are grouped according to yearly themes. You may choose to include a favorite piece of children's literature that is appropriate for your yearly theme. The Christmas and Hanukkah books listed represent a variety of titles that may be offered as student selections during December.

Year 1

Soup. Robert Newton Peck. Dell, 1974.
The Matchlock Gun. Walter S. Edmonds. Troll, 1990.
Early Thunder. Jean Fritz. Puffin, 1987.
The Cabin Faced West. Jean Fritz. Puffin, 1987.
The Perilous Road. William O. Steele. Harcourt Brace, 1990.
The House of Wings. Betsy Byars. Puffin, 1982.
Island of the Blue Dolphins. Scott O'Dell. Dell, 1960.

Year 2

My Father's Dragon. Ruth Gannett. Random House, 1948.
The Buffalo Knife. William O. Steele. Harcourt Brace, 1990.
Luke Was There. Eleanor Clymer. Peter Smith, 1992.
Dear Mr. Henshaw. Beverly Cleary. Dell, 1983.
Night of the Twisters. Ivy Ruckman. Harper, 1984.

Year 3

The Midnight Fox. Betsy Byars. Scholastic, 1968.
Naya Nuki: Shoshoni Girl Who Ran. Kenneth Thomasma. Baker, 1991.
Stone Fox. John Reynolds Gardiner. Trumpet Club, 1980.
Number the Stars. Lois Lowry. Dell, 1989.
In the Year of the Boar and Jackie Robinson. Bette Bao Lord. Trumpet Club, 1984.

Christmas Books

The After-Christmas Tree. Linda Wagner Tyler. Penguin, 1990.
The Best Christmas Pageant Ever. Barbara Robinson. Trumpet Club, 1972.
A Certain Small Shepherd. Rebecca Caudill. Henry Holt & Co., 1987.
The Christmas Dolls. Carol Beach York. Scholastic, 1967.
A Christmas Sonata. Gary Paulsen. Dell, 1992.
The Christmas Spurs. Bill Wallace. Pocket Books, 1990.
The Christmas Tree That Ate My Mother. Dean Marney. Scholastic, 1992.
December Secrets. Patricia Giff. Dell, 1984.
Goliath's Christmas. Terrance Dicks. Scholastic, 1986.
The Jingle Bells Jam. Patricia Giff. Dell, 1992.
The Lion in the Box. Marguerite de Angeli. Dell, 1975.
Merry Christmas, Miss McConnell! Colleen O'Shaughnessy McKenna. Scholastic, 1990.
Other Bells For Us To Ring. Robert Cormier. Dell, 1990.
Tis the Season: Holiday Stories. Highlights. Boyds Mills, 1993.
The Worst Christmas Ever. Connie Remlinger-Trounstine. Troll,1994.

Hanukkah Books

The Spotted Pony: A Collection of Hanukkah Stories. Holiday, 1992.
The Power of Light. Issac Bashevis Singer. Avon, 1980.
Hanukkah, Eight Lights around the World. Whitman, 1988.
The Story of Hanukkah. Illustrated by Ori Sherman. Dial 1989.
Hershel and the Hanukkah Goblins. Eric Kimmel. Holiday, 1989.

Sample Year-Long Theme: Year 1, Getting Organized

The following pages provide a curriculum framework for each year of the three-year cycle. Following the outline for each year is a set of literature based unit webs. The webs provide a concise layout of possible subject areas and skills related to and integrated with the selected piece of literature.

August/September: Getting Organized as a Child

- **Literature:** *Soup* by Robert Newton Peck
- **Language Arts Focus:** literature activities, writing assessment criteria, descriptive paragraphs, story elements, plot, adjectives, nouns, words emersion (root words, origin, prefix, suffix), dictionary skills, autobiographies
- **Math Focus:** populations, graphing, measurement, time
- **Integrated Subject Areas:** parts of a book, problem solving, science experiments, discussions, tables and charts, following directions

October: Events That Stimulated Exploration

- **Literature:** Social Studies Textbook
- **Language Arts Focus:** oral reporting, narrative writing, focus on descriptive details of a story in reading and writing, main idea, comprehension, predictions
- **Math Focus:** decimals, money, checkbooks
- **Integrated Subject Areas:** trade, exploration, Vikings, identifying continents, major countries and bodies of water, and map skills

November: Getting Organized as a Young Country

- **Literature:** *Early Thunder* by Jean Fritz; also include *The Matchlock Gun* and *Johnny Tremain*
- **Language Arts Focus:** cursive handwriting, friendly letters, fact vs. fiction, verbs, syllables, pronouns, cause and effect, compound words, descriptive writing, literature discussion group, focus on descriptive details of a story in reading and writing
- **Math Focus:** time, operations, and computation
- **Integrated Subject Areas:** Revolutionary War, three branches of government, the Constitution, Declaration of Independence, political parties (Whig and Tory), Intolerable Acts, health, Samuel Adams and other leaders

December: Getting Organized as the Country Expands Westward

- **Literature:** *The Cabin Faced West* by Jean Fritz
- **Language Arts Focus:** writing paragraphs, types of sentences, subject/predicate agreement, figurative language, poetry, proper nouns, dialect, capitalization

Sample Year-Long Theme: Year 1, Getting Organized *(cont.)*

- **Math Focus:** numeration, patterns
- **Integrated Subject Areas:** geology, rocks and minerals, westward expansion, U.S. landforms, natural resources, pioneer crafts, mapping skills

January: Getting Organized as a Country during the Civil War

- **Literature:** *The Perilous Road* by William O. Steele
- **Language Arts Focus:** dialogue in student writing, paragraphs, research, proper nouns, historical fiction, process, or "how-to" paper, words to use instead of "said," outlining, prefixes and suffixes, synonyms/antonyms
- **Math Focus:** fractions, probability
- **Integrated Subject Areas:** Civil War history, rebuilding; recognizing trees, nuts, and wildflowers: hunting; wagons; folk tales; cliff hangers; riddles; pioneer crafts

February: Industrial Revolution

- **Literature:** biographies of inventors
- **Language Arts Focus:** author's purpose, reference skills, informative articles, punctuation, public speaking, commas, main idea, biography
- **Math Focus:** geometry
- **Integrated Subject Areas:** inventions, simple machines, tangrams

March/April: Getting Organized as an Animal

- **Literature:** *The House of Wings* by Betsy Byars
- **Language Arts Focus:** possessive, contractions, similes, verbs, descriptive writing, sequence, adjectives, subject-verb agreement, legends
- **Math Focus:** measurement
- **Integrated Subject Areas:** insects, habitats, birds, advertisements, propaganda

May: Getting Organized as an Animal

- **Literature:** *The Island of the Blue Dolphins* by Scott O'Dell or *The Big Wave* by Pearl S. Buck
- **Language Arts Focus:** comparisons, descriptive writing, "how-to" papers, webbing, adverbs, folktales
- **Math Focus:** problem solving, probability, measurement
- **Integrated Subject Areas:** oceanography, ocean resources, animal research, vertibrates and invertebrates, weather, classifying shells and fish

Thematic Unit Web Form

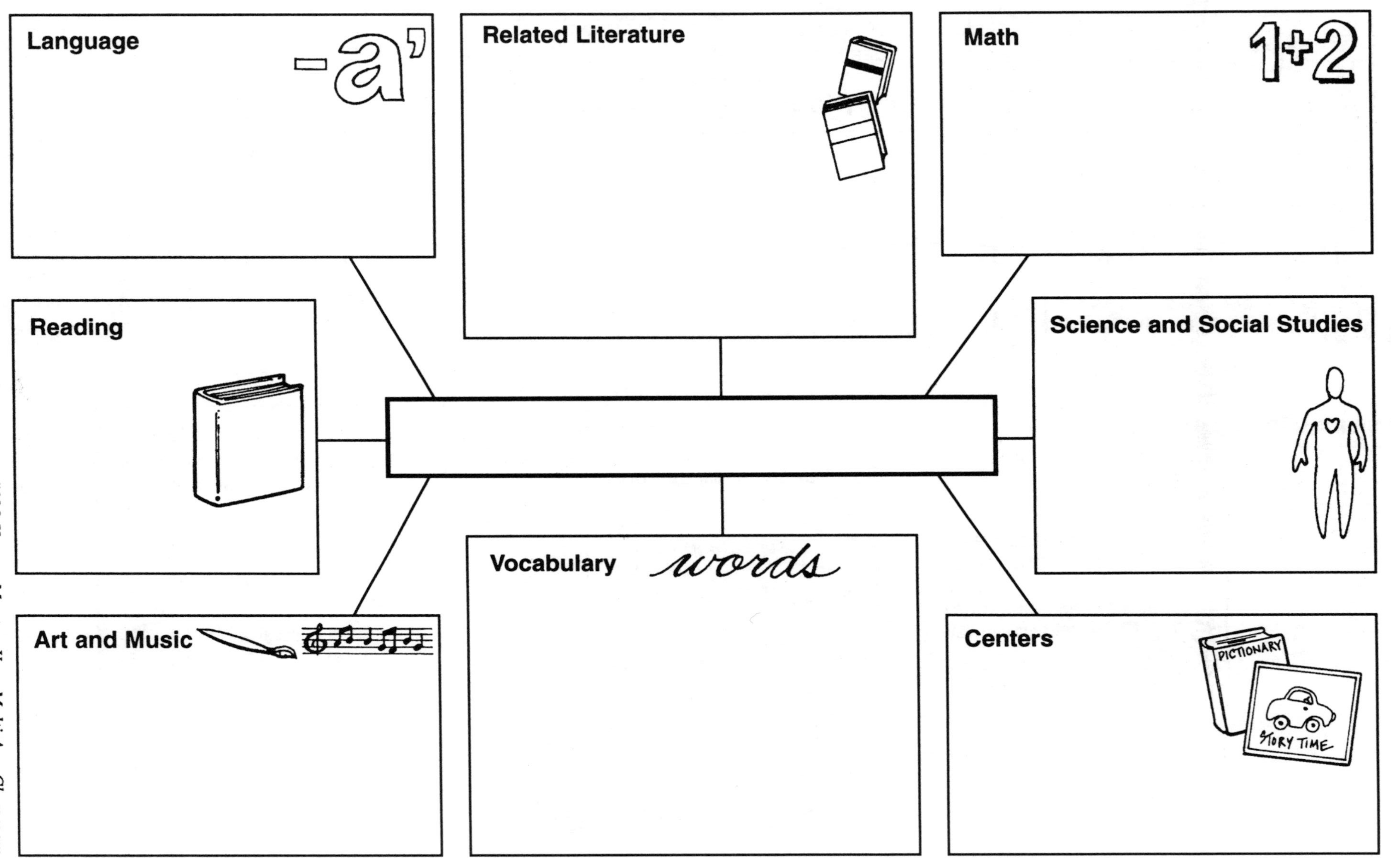

Soup Unit Web

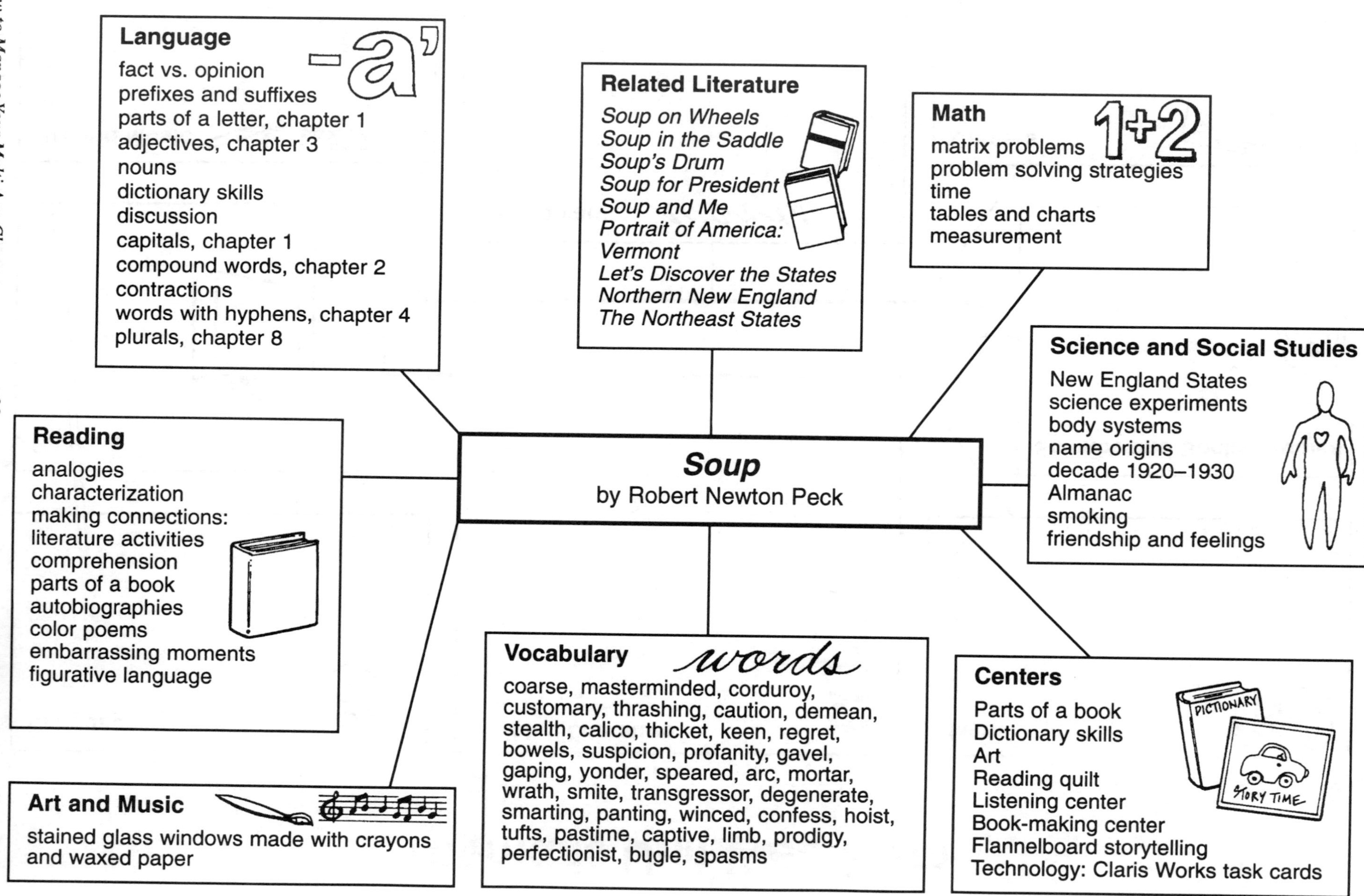

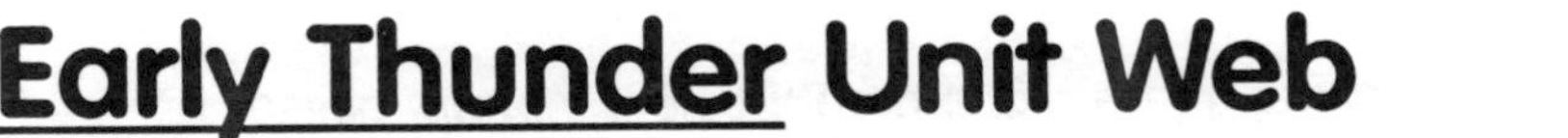

Early Thunder Unit Web

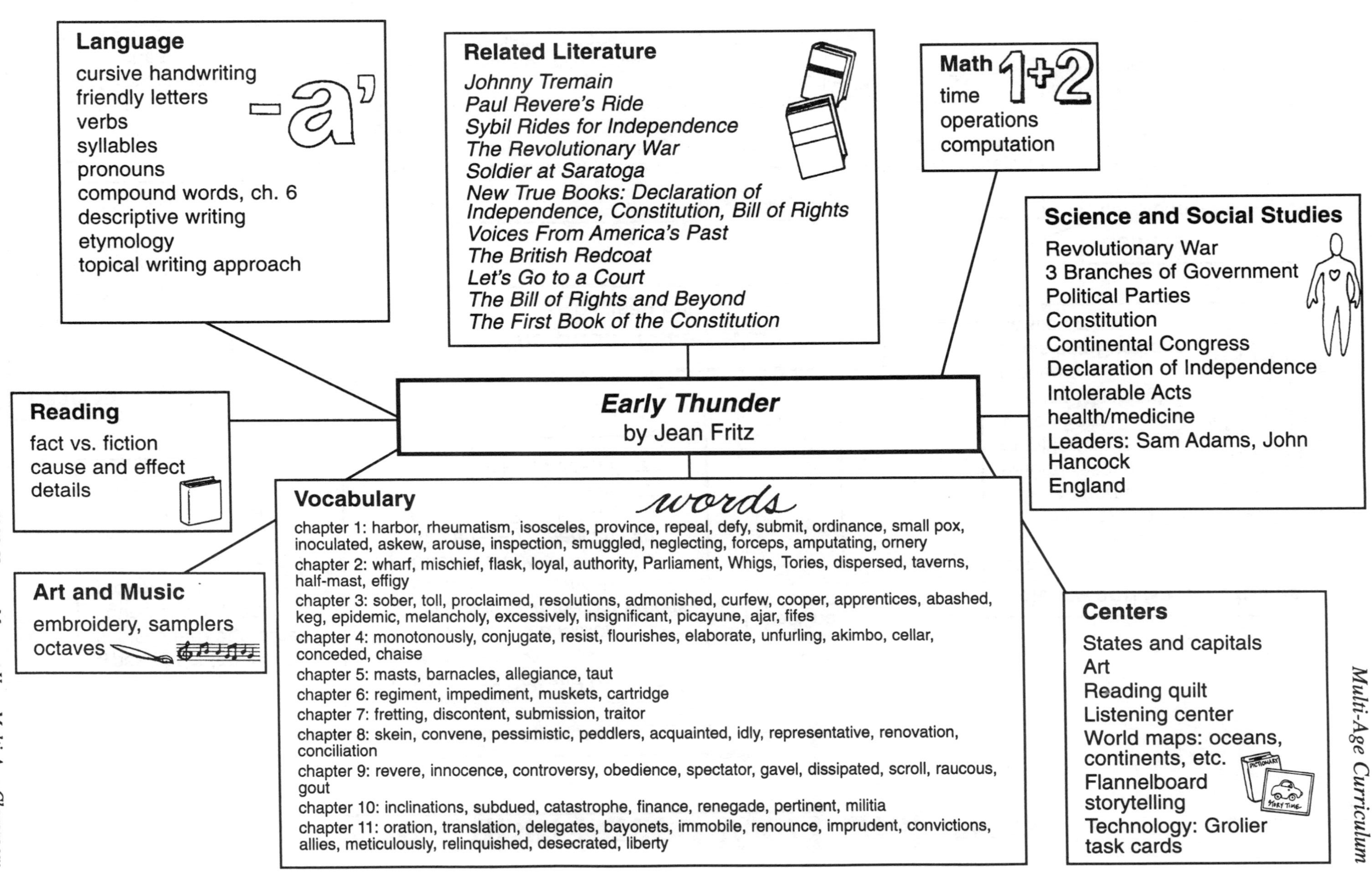

The Cabin Faced West Unit Web

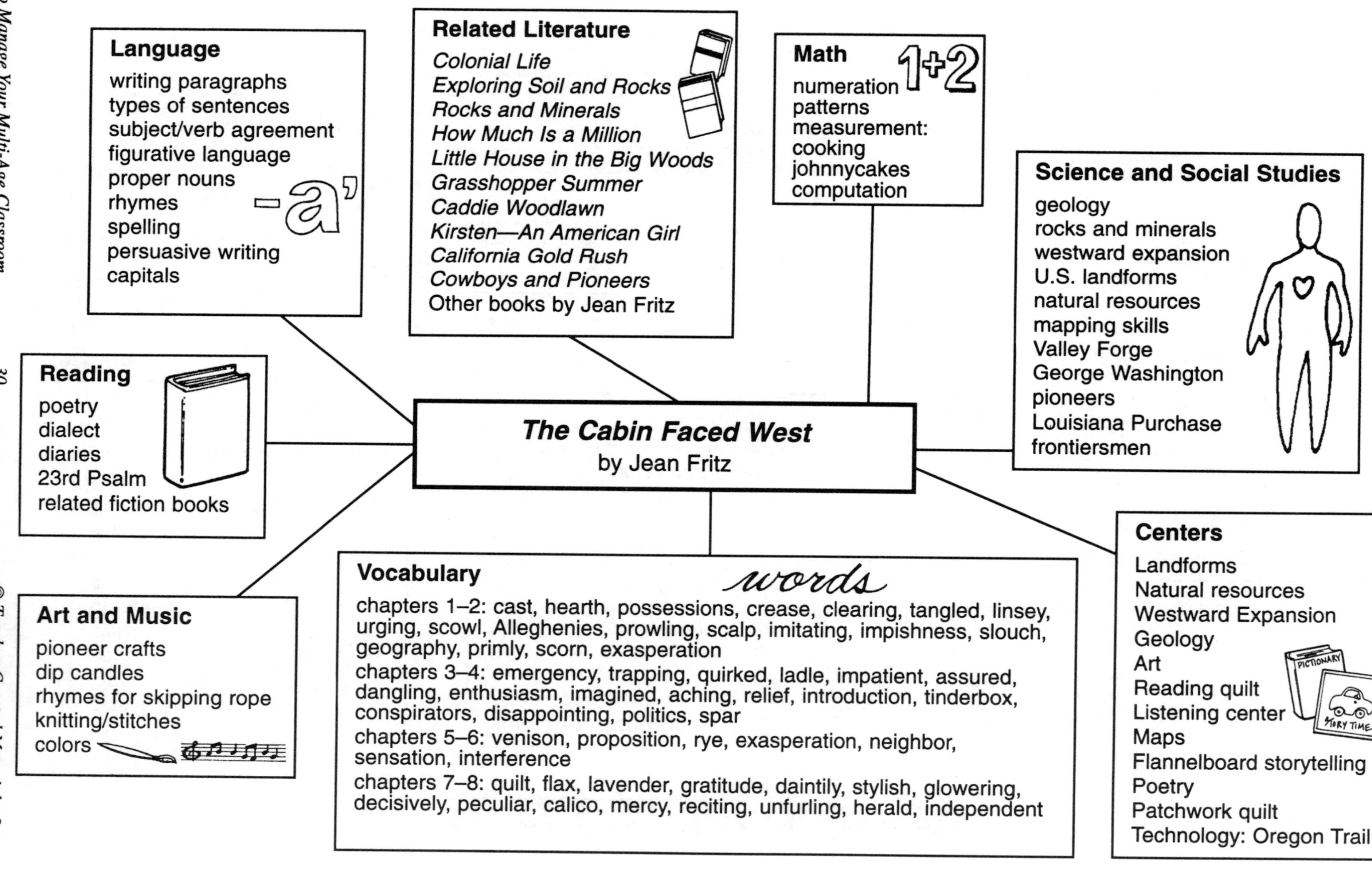

The Perilous Road Unit Web

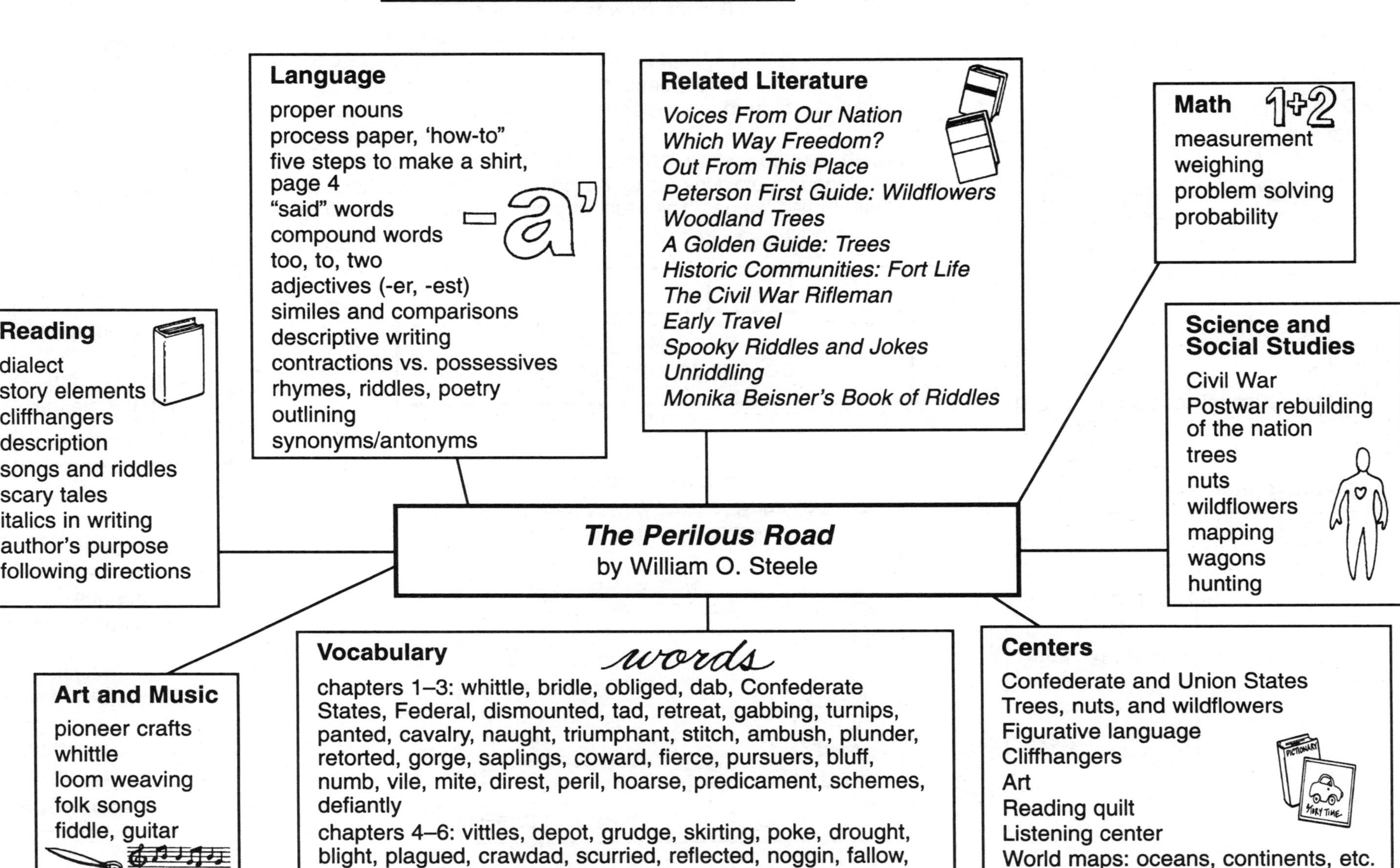

The House of Wings Unit Web

The House of Wings
by Betsy Byars

Language
possession
contractions
similies
descriptive writing
adjectives
verbs
subject/verb agreement
application for job
hyphens

Related Literature
Eyewitness Books: Insect
Eyewitness Books: Bird
Insects
Owls
Birds and Their Nests
Eyewitness Juniors
Amazing Birds
The Big Golden Book of Backyard Birds
Action Science—Birds
What Is a Bird?
How to Be a Nature Detective
Experiments With Animal Behavior
Other books by Betsy Byars

Math
fractions
weight
measurement
probability

Reading
advertisements
grocery products
sequence
legends

Science and Social Studies
insects
habitats
birds: geese, owls, canaries, parrots
Ohio
sight

Art and Music
"I've Been Working on the Railroad"
pencil drawings of classroom pets

Vocabulary
chapters 1–3: culvert, median, unwieldy, canary, disgraceful, croquet, peacock, unsuspecting, buoy, suspicion, sneer, concentrated, asphalt, bare, hesitated, wailed, peered, glared, miniature, urgency, brow

chapters 4–6: mites, foliage, comforting, migrating, lightheaded, gnat, intensity, fatigue, poised, proceeded

chapters 7–10: cranes, perch, serpentine, wheezing, magnified, yonder, sagged, jovial, cackling, spigot, persistent, agitation, anxiety, sloshed, mocking, porcelain, stoking, gazing

chapters 11–14: banister, periscope, inattentive, rebelled, gullet, fragile, tidier, talons, judgment, hygiene, grubs, confirmation, intense

Centers
Propaganda in commercials (see homework)
Birds
Habitats
Art
Reading quilt
Listening center
World maps: oceans, continents, etc.
Bookmaking center
Flannelboard storytelling
Technology

Island of the Blue Dolphins Unit Web

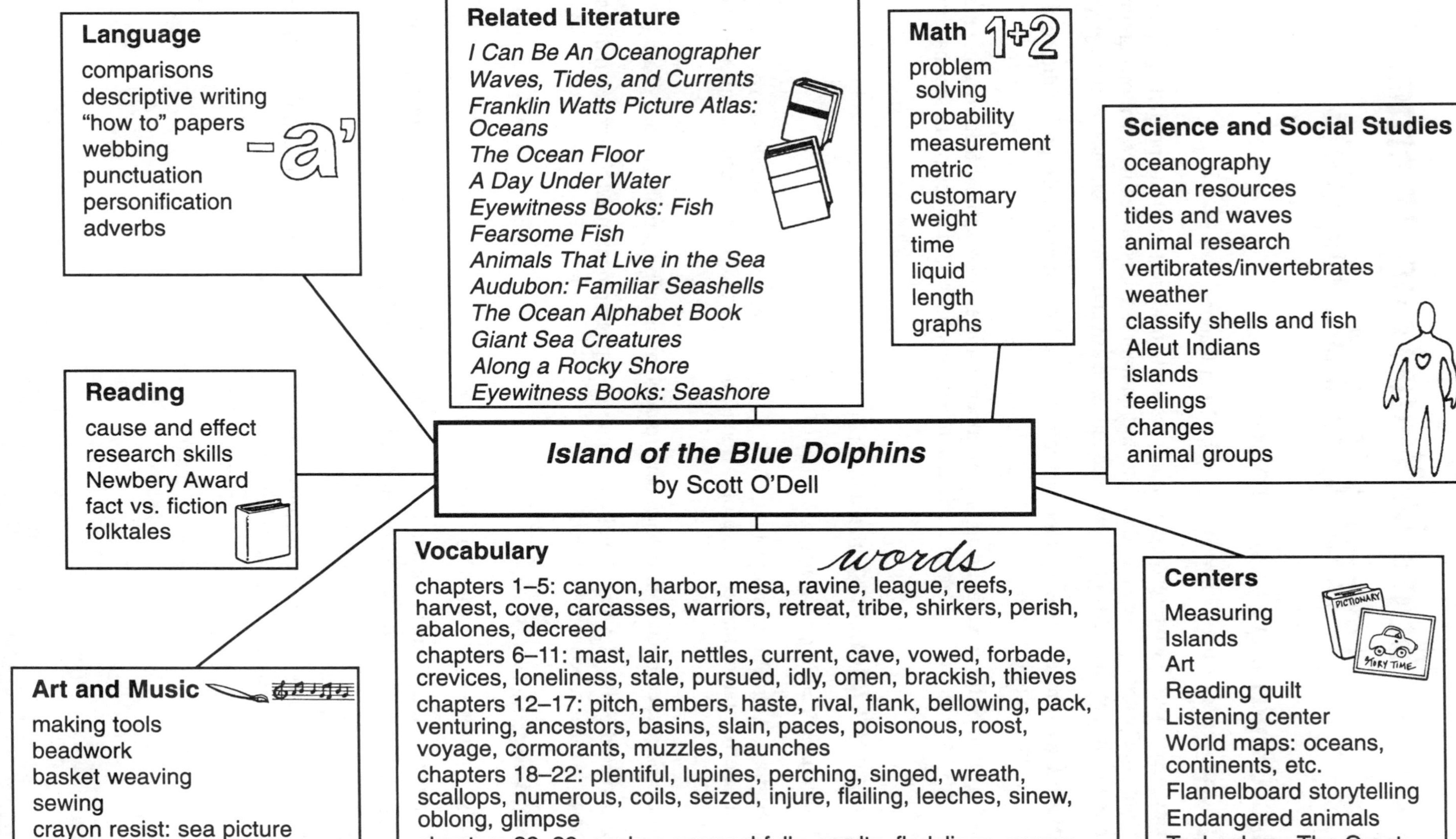

Sample Year-Long Theme: Year 2, U.S.A. Regions

August/September: Islands and Oceans

- **Literature:** *My Father's Dragon* series by Ruth Gannett
- **Language Arts Focus:** reading, writing, research, resources, editing, predicting, contractions, compound words, possession, dialogue and quotation marks, adjectives, following directions, retelling directions, parts of a book, sequence, cause and effect, commas, autobiography
- **Math Focus:** measurement, graphing, coordinates, Roman numerals, probability, ordinals, operations, computation
- **Integrated Subject Areas:** mapping, weather, climate, geographical features (mountains, caves, islands, volcanoes), endangered animals, health, continents, clay sculpture, drama, crayon resist, mixing colors

September/October: Southeastern States

- **Literature:** *The Buffalo Knife* by William O. Steele
- **Language Arts Focus:** storytelling (Jack Tales), legends, adverbs, dialects, vocabulary, characterization, capitalization, proper nouns, nouns, word parts (prefixes, suffixes, base words), syllables
- **Math Focus:** computation, independent folders, numeration, graphs, tables, charts
- **Integrated Subject Areas:** Smoky Mountains, topographical maps, Cherokee Indians, Appalachian history, change, economy, mapping

November: Major U.S. cities

- **Literature:** *Luke Was There* by Eleanor Clymer
- **Language Arts Focus:** pronouns, complete sentences, subject/verb agreement, cursive handwriting, sequencing, verbs, outlines, dictionary skills, synonyms/antonyms
- **Math Focus:** money, decimals, time
- **Integrated Subject Areas:** museums, bridges, city services (ambulance, police, children's home), homelessness, feelings, human behavior

Sample Year-Long Theme: Year 2, U.S.A. Regions *(cont.)*

December: Christmas Across the U.S.A.

- **Literature:** Christmas Novels—Student Choice
- **Language Arts Focus:** figurative language, details, main idea, predicting, comprehension, narrative writing, story elements, plot, Christmas book project, oral reporting
- **Math Focus:** geometry, decimals, money, checkbooks, patterns
- **Integrated Subject Areas:** gingerbread houses, human body, nutrition

January: Pacific States

- **Literature:** *Dear Mr. Henshaw* by Beaverly Cleary
- **Language Arts Focus:** letter writing, parts of friendly letters, paragraphs, author's purpose, publishing stories and books, story mapping, sequence, biographies, punctuation, adjectives
- **Math Focus:** cost of electrical supplies, magic squares, cooking, fractions, menus
- **Integrated Subject Areas:** magnetism and electricity, road maps, telephone skills, bakeries, Ben Franklin, feelings, economy

February/March: State Partner Projects

- **Literature:** Reference Materials and Informational Books: addresses for the Department of Tourism for each state are provided as a resource to use with this particular unit. Students may be divided into partner groups and be assigned a state to research and write to.
- **Language Arts Focus:** Multi-Age play performance, letter writing, addressing envelopes, card catalog, research and reference materials, oral presentations (public speaking), capitalization, informative articles
- **Math Focus:** averaging, numeration, rounding, estimating
- **Integrated Subject Areas:** video taping, symbols, creating visuals, mapping, sound, heat, light

April/May: Central Plains States

- **Literature:** *Night of the Twisters* by Ivy Ruckman
- **Language Arts Focus:** story elements (setting, plot, characterization, theme, conclusion), illustrations, story mapping, fact vs. fiction, commas, reports
- **Math Focus:** geometry, area, perimeter, problem solving
- **Integrated Subject Areas:** community helpers, severe weather, propaganda, climate

Free State Brochures and Information

The addresses on the following page are included with Year 2: U.S.A. Regions. Instead of planning every unit around a piece of literature, plan a time during the second half of Year 2 for students to research and report upon an assigned state. Students may work individually or be assigned a partner. Each of the fifty states should be included, or at least one state from each region. Students should write a letter to the Office of Tourism for their states, requesting free information and brochures.

Final reports should include a three to five minute oral presentation communicating at least five facts about the state, visuals, and bibliography for three resources used. Final report presentations may be videotaped. During this unit, classes may also study American landmarks, major rivers, a timeline of when states joined the U.S.A., populations of states, and natural resources. This type of unit lends itself toward having a performance about the fifty states as a culminating activity to communicate with parents.

Addresses are from State Administrative Officials by the Council of State Governments. Lexington, KY: 1992

Map of Regional Literature

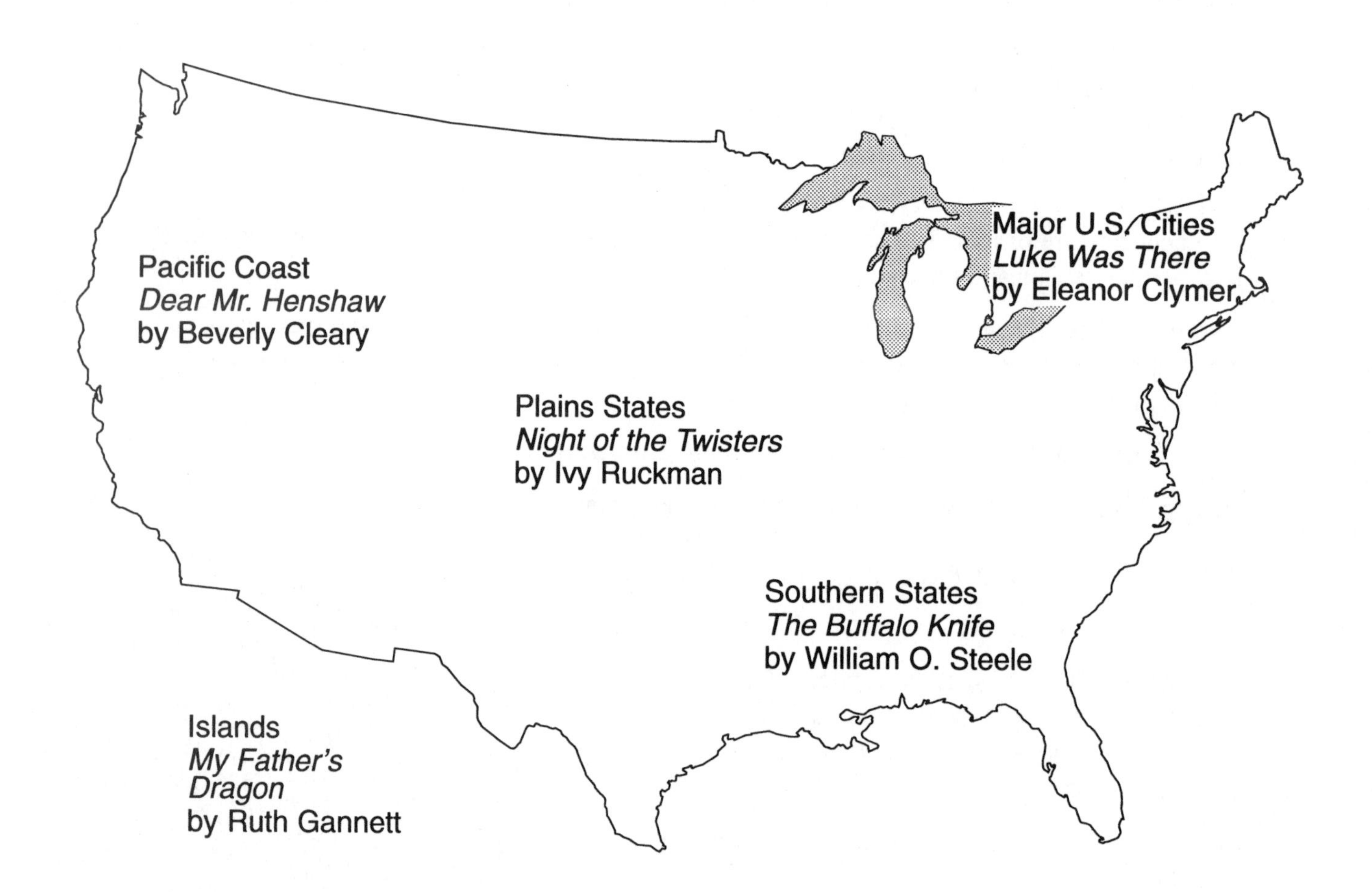

Addresses for Free State Brochures and Information

ALABAMA
401 Adams Ave., Ste. 126
Montgomery, AL 36104

ALASKA
P.O. Box 110810
Juneau, AK 99811

ARIZONA
1100 W. Washington
Phoenix, AZ 85007

ARKANSAS
One Capital Mall
Little Rock, AR 72201

CALIFORNIA
801 K Street, Ste. 1600
Sacramento, CA 95814

COLORADO
5500 Greenwood Plaza Blvd., #200
Englewood, CO 80111

CONNECTICUT
865 Brook Street
Rocky Hill, CT 06067

DELAWARE
P.O. Box 1401
Dover, DE 19901

FLORIDA
Collins Building, Rm 511
107 W. Gaines Street
Tallahassee, FL 32399-2000

GEORGIA
285 Peachtree Ctr. Ave., #1000
Atlanta, GA 30303

HAWAII
220 S. King St., #1100
Honolulu, HI 96813

IDAHO
700 W. State St.
Boise, ID 83720

ILLINOIS
620 E. Adams St., 3rd Fl.
Springfield, IL 62701

INDIANA
1 N. Capitol
Indianapolis, IN 46204

IOWA
200 E. Grand
Des Moines, IA 50309

KANSAS
700 SW Harrison Ave., Ste. 1300
Topeka, KS 66612-3712

KENTUCKY
Capital Plaza Tower, 24th Fl.
Frankfort, KY 40601

LOUISIANA
P.O. Box 94291
Baton Rouge, LA 70804

MAINE
State House Station #59
Augusta, ME 04333

MARYLAND
217 E. Redwood Street
Baltimore, MD 21201

MASSACHUSETTS
100 Cambridge St., 13th Fl.
Boston, MA 02202

MICHIGAN
333 S. Capitol Ave.
Lansing, MI 48909

MINNESOTA
100 Metro Sq. Bldg., 121 7th Pl., E.
St. Paul, MN 55101

MISSISSIPPI
P.O. Box 849
Jackson, MS 39205

MISSOURI
Truman Bldg., Rm 290
Jefferson City, MO 65102

MONTANA
1424 Ninth Avenue
Helena, MT 59620

NEBRASKA
P.O. Box 94666
Lincoln, NE 68509

NEVADA
5151 S. Carson St.
Carson City, NV 89710

NEW HAMPSHIRE
172 Pembroke Rd.
Concord, NH 03301

NEW JERSEY
20 W. State St., CN 826
Trenton, NJ 08625

NEW MEXICO
1100 St. Francis Drive
Santa Fe, NM 87503

NEW YORK
1 Commerce Plaza
Albany, NY 12245

NORTH CAROLINA
430 N. Salisbury St.
Raleigh, NC 27603

NORTH DAKOTA
Liberty Memorial Bldg.
604 E. Blvd. Ave
Bismark, ND 58505-0662

OHIO
30 E. Broad St., 25th Fl.
Columbus, OH 43266

OKLAHOMA
500 Will Rodgers Bldg.
Oklahoma City, OK 73105

OREGON
775 Summer St.
Salem, OR 97310

PENNSYLVANIA
433 Forum Bldg.
Harrisburg, PA 17120

RHODE ISLAND
7 Jackson Walkway
Providence, RI 02903

SOUTH CAROLINA
1205 Pendleton St.
Columbia, SC 29201

SOUTH DAKOTA
Capitol Lake Plaza
Pierre, SD 57501

TENNESSEE
320 Sixth Ave., North
Nashville, TN 37243

TEXAS
P.O. Box 12728
Austin, TX 78711

UTAH
Council Hall and Capitol Hill
Salt Lake City, UT 84114

VERMONT
134 State Street
Montpelier, VT 05602

VIRGINIA
West Tower – 19th Fl.
901 E. Byrd St.
Richmond, VA 23219

WASHINGTON
P.O. Box 42500
Olympia, WA 98504-2500

WEST VIRGINIA
State Capitol Complex
Bldg. 6, Rm. 451
1900 Kanawha Blvd. E.
Charleston, WV 25305-0312

WISCONSIN
P.O. Box 7970, 123 W. Washington
Madison, WI 53707

WYOMING
I-25 at College Dr.
Cheyenne, WY 82002

My Father's Dragon Series Unit Web

My Father's Dragon Series
by Ruth Styles Gannett

Language

contractions
adjectives
compound words
chapter 1: Interview father/male
persuade mom to keep the cat
flannelboard storytelling:
page 178: Counting Crocodiles
page 201: Monkey and Crocodile
process writing
chapter 2: How to Make a Peanut Butter and Jelly Sandwich
chapter 6: Debate importance of brushing teeth
20 Questions–guess items in a box by feeling and asking questions

Related Literature

The Little Island
The 14th Dragon
The Search for the Ten-Winged Dragon
The Last of the Dragons
A Good Knight for Dragons
The Enormous Crocodile
The Birth of an Island
Island of the Oceans
A First Look at Seashells
The Reluctant Dragon
Jack and the Fire Dragon
World Atlas
Animals, Animals

Math

classifying objects
numeration
graphing
measurement
ordinals
Roman numerals
probability

Science and Social Studies

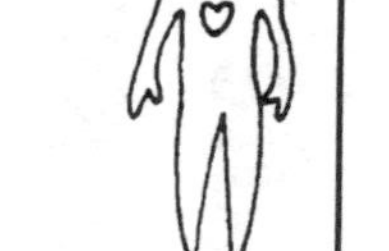

how islands are formed
volcanoes
jungle environment
endangered animals
camouflage
animal adaptations
landforms: islands, continents, oceans, rivers
Hawaii

Reading

predicting
reading for details
sequencing
literature for information and pleasure
Reading Response
predict contents of knapsack
compose a "missing person" ad or news article
animal webbing
brainstorming solutions
write a sequel

Vocabulary

chapter 1: obliged, apologized, cellar, port, tangerine, weep
chapter 2: inconvenient, crocodiles, dependable, stake, miserable, docks, rescue, knapsack, distract
chapter 3: cargo, merchant, punctual
chapter 4: solemn, boulders, unreliable, trundled
chapter 5: gloomy, dense, compass, trespass, contradict, curious, scarce
chapter 6: rhinoceros
chapter 7: prancing, mane, allowance, forelock
chapter 8: dignified, fierce, enormous, magnify
chapter 9: summon
chapter 10: screech, bellow

Art and Music

clay sculptures of animals
crayon resist
animal pop-ups
dragon puppetry
Oceans audiotape

Centers

Dragon Math: problem solving, graphing
Islands: name, locate, graph
Classifying seashells
Volcanoes: research and build
Art
Puppetry
Endangered animals
Reading quilt
Listening center
Oceans
World maps: oceans, continents, etc.
Flannelboard storytelling
Poetry: writing and publishing
Technology: Grolier cards

The Buffalo Knife Unit Web

The Buffalo Knife
by William O. Steele

Language
plurals
possessive nouns
card catalogue
Acrostic/Ladder poems
dialogue writing
research
dialect
adverbs

Reading
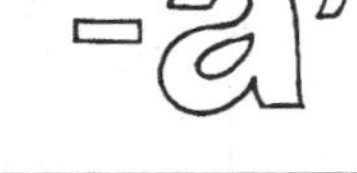
author's purpose
comprehension
cause and effect
riddles
famous Appalachian people
legends: Jack Tales

Art and Music
Appalachian instruments
make homemade instruments
candle making
cornhusk dolls
cross-stitch
weaving
painting
whittling—wood carving
songs:
"Rocky Top"
"Dixie"
"Tennessee Waltz"

Related Literature
Portrait of America: Tennessee
Jack Tales
Biographies of Famous Tennesseans
Eyewitness Books: Trees
A Golden Guide: Trees
The History of the Trail of Tears
The Cherokee
Pioneer Children of Appalachia
Indian Signals and Sign Language
Let's Discover: Southeast

Math
population task cards
graph of city populations
place value
numeration
tables and charts
computation

Science and Social Studies

southeastern U.S. history
southeastern states map
topographical maps
natural resources
Native Americans: Cherokee
Venn Diagram of 3 presidents
tree identification
extinct/endangered animals
regional economy
Progress
Smoky Mountains

Vocabulary
chapters 1–4: catamount, scabbard, soberly, savannahs, solemnly, shoals, tote, sullenly, feisty, mournfully, hearth, trencher, pondered

chapters 5–7: tethered, timidly, torment, dismay, foe, haunch, endurance, stern, quailed, flinch, dugouts, riled, scanned, tartly, cowered, twilight, grimaced, gasp, halt, rouse, reflection, pallet

chapters 8–10: heedless, compresses, sieve, rouse, reluctant, merchant, cascaded, askew, hastily, rapids, starvation, murmured, despair, nuisance, ponder, desolate

Centers
Salt dough map depicting region of literature
Regions
Topographical maps
Regional products
Regional scavenger hunt
Regional trees
Art
Reading quilt
Listening center
World maps: oceans, continents, etc.
Flannelboard storytelling
Technology

Luke Was There Unit Web

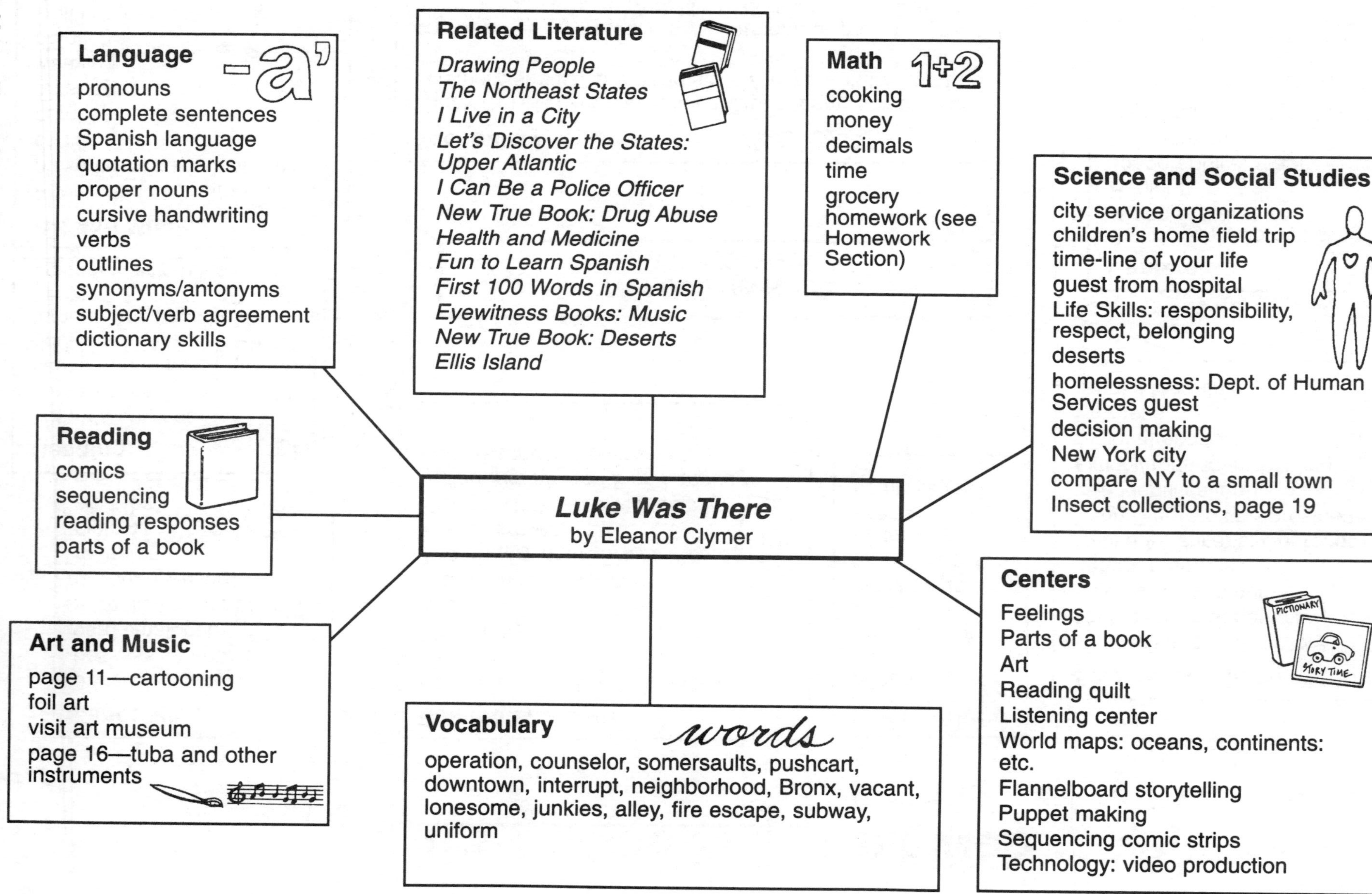

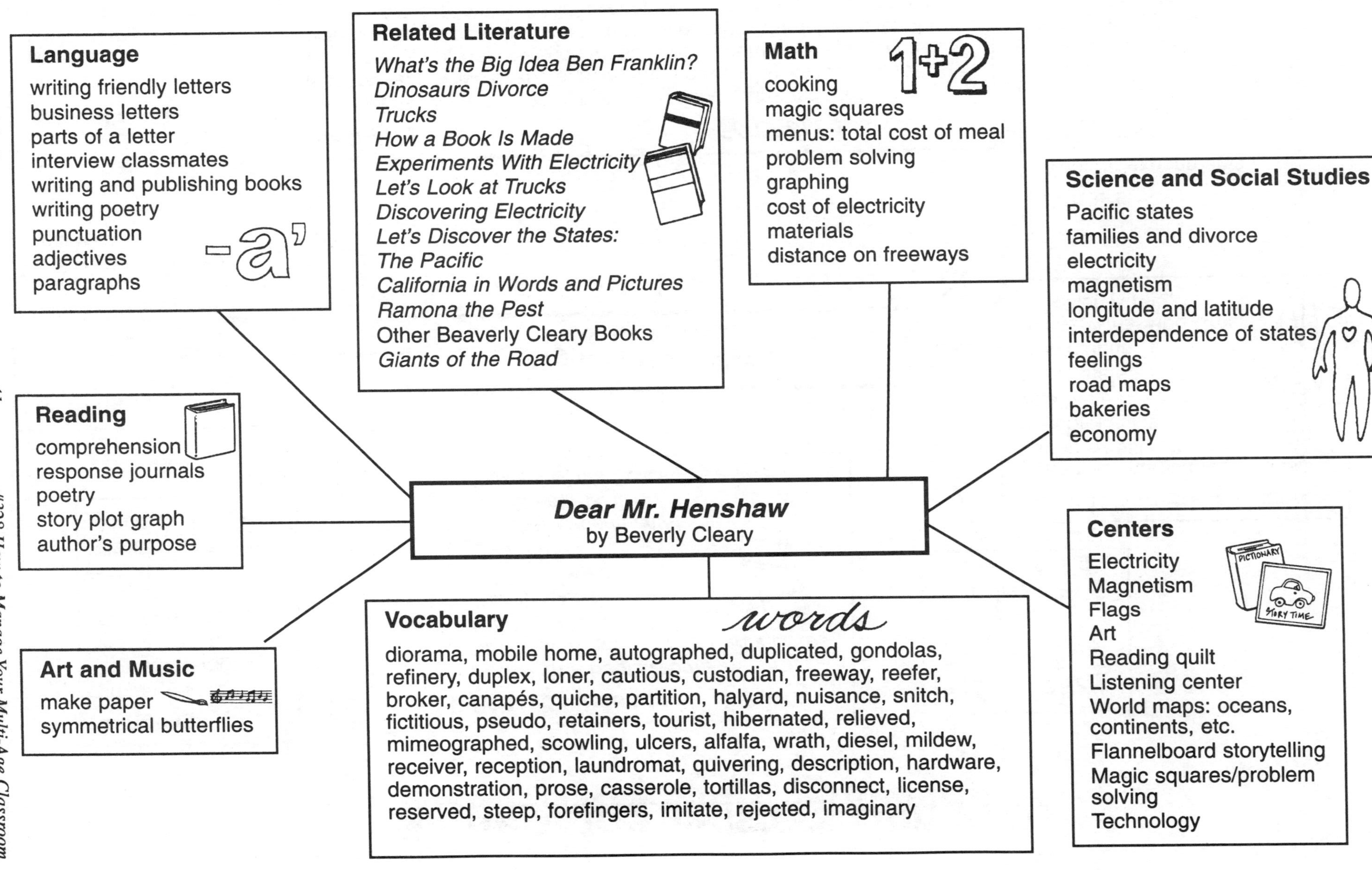
Dear Mr. Henshaw Unit Web
Dear Mr. Henshaw
by Beverly Cleary
Language
writing friendly letters
business letters
parts of a letter
interview classmates
writing and publishing books
writing poetry
punctuation
adjectives
paragraphs
-a'
Related Literature
What's the Big Idea Ben Franklin?
Dinosaurs Divorce
Trucks
How a Book Is Made
Experiments With Electricity
Let's Look at Trucks
Discovering Electricity
Let's Discover the States:
The Pacific
California in Words and Pictures
Ramona the Pest
Other Beaverly Cleary Books
Giants of the Road
Math
1+2
cooking
magic squares
menus: total cost of meal
problem solving
graphing
cost of electricity
materials
distance on freeways
Science and Social Studies
Pacific states
families and divorce
electricity
magnetism
longitude and latitude
interdependence of states
feelings
road maps
bakeries
economy
Reading
comprehension
response journals
poetry
story plot graph
author's purpose
Art and Music
make paper
symmetrical butterflies
Vocabulary
words
diorama, mobile home, autographed, duplicated, gondolas, refinery, duplex, loner, cautious, custodian, freeway, reefer, broker, canapés, quiche, partition, halyard, nuisance, snitch, fictitious, pseudo, retainers, tourist, hibernated, relieved, mimeographed, scowling, ulcers, alfalfa, wrath, diesel, mildew, receiver, reception, laundromat, quivering, description, hardware, demonstration, prose, casserole, tortillas, disconnect, license, reserved, steep, forefingers, imitate, rejected, imaginary
Centers
Electricity
Magnetism
Flags
Art
Reading quilt
Listening center
World maps: oceans, continents, etc.
Flannelboard storytelling
Magic squares/problem solving
Technology
PICTIONARY
STORY TIME

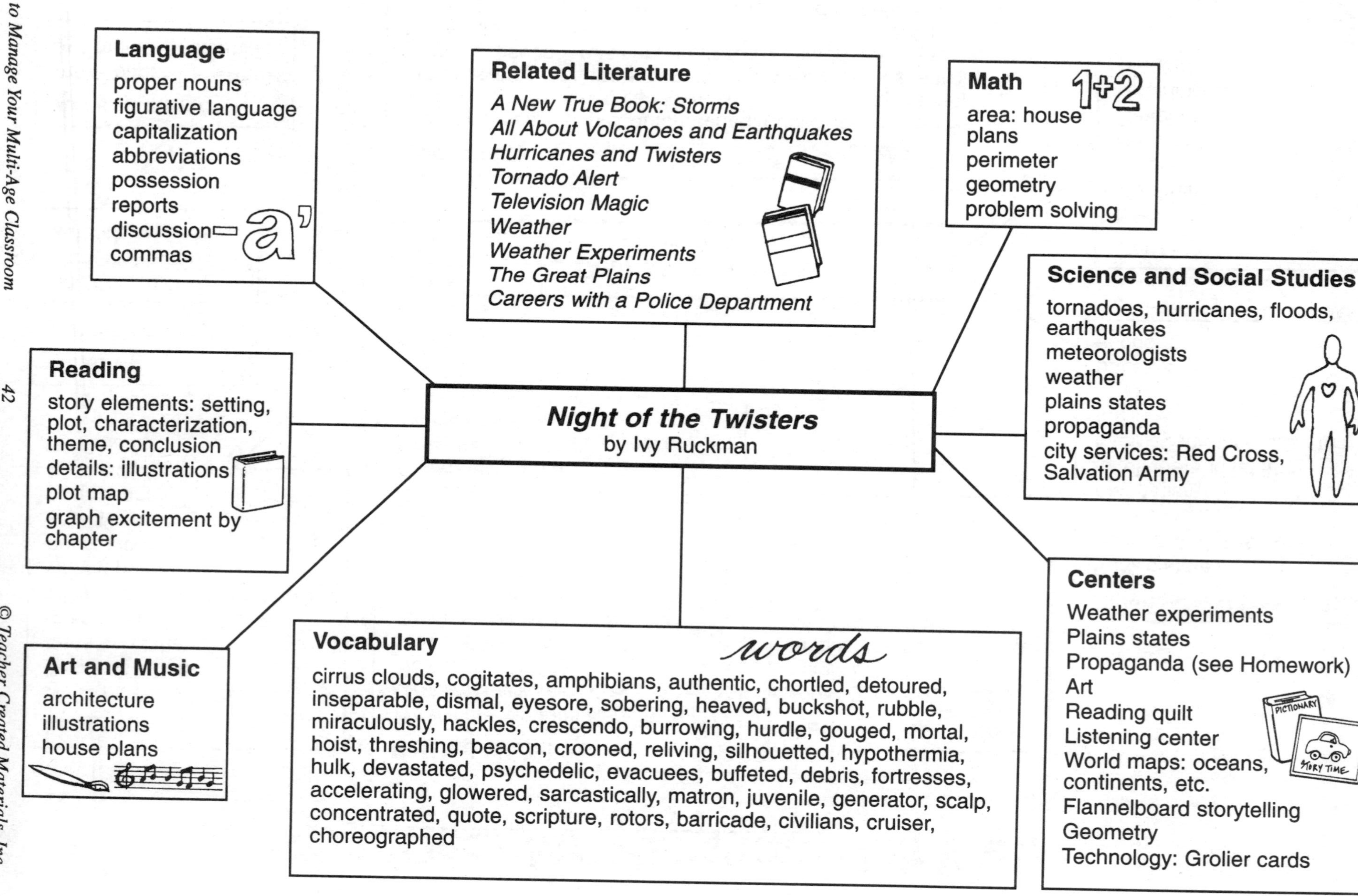
Night of the Twisters Unit Web
Language
proper nouns
figurative language
capitalization
abbreviations
possession
reports
discussion
commas
Related Literature
A New True Book: Storms
All About Volcanoes and Earthquakes
Hurricanes and Twisters
Tornado Alert
Television Magic
Weather
Weather Experiments
The Great Plains
Careers with a Police Department
Math
area: house plans
perimeter
geometry
problem solving
Science and Social Studies
tornadoes, hurricanes, floods, earthquakes
meteorologists
weather
plains states
propaganda
city services: Red Cross, Salvation Army
Reading
story elements: setting, plot, characterization, theme, conclusion
details: illustrations
plot map
graph excitement by chapter
Night of the Twisters
by Ivy Ruckman
Art and Music
architecture
illustrations
house plans
Vocabulary
words
cirrus clouds, cogitates, amphibians, authentic, chortled, detoured, inseparable, dismal, eyesore, sobering, heaved, buckshot, rubble, miraculously, hackles, crescendo, burrowing, hurdle, gouged, mortal, hoist, threshing, beacon, crooned, reliving, silhouetted, hypothermia, hulk, devastated, psychedelic, evacuees, buffeted, debris, fortresses, accelerating, glowered, sarcastically, matron, juvenile, generator, scalp, concentrated, quote, scripture, rotors, barricade, civilians, cruiser, choreographed
Centers
Weather experiments
Plains states
Propaganda (see Homework)
Art
Reading quilt
Listening center
World maps: oceans, continents, etc.
Flannelboard storytelling
Geometry
Technology: Grolier cards
PICTIONARY
STORY TIME

Sample Year-Long Theme: Year 3, Communities

August/September: Farm Communities

- **Literature:** *The Midnight Fox* by Betsy Byars
- **Language Arts Focus:** predicting, contractions, compounds, possession dialogue, adjectives, following directions, retelling directions, parts of a book, sequence, words for "said" (responded, related, remarked), nouns, autobiography
- **Math Focus:** graphs, money, measurement, coordinates, grids, operations, computation
- **Integrated Subject Areas:** plants and seeds, bees, local and state governments

October/November: Native American communities

- **Literature:** *Naya Nuki: Shoshoni Girl Who Ran* by Kenneth Thomasma
- **Language Arts Focus:** problem solving, prediction, adverbs, adjectives, verbs, figurative language, plurals, homonyms, possession, "how-to" papers, Native American tales, friendly letters
- **Math Focus:** number words, fractions, measurement, distance, estimating, pumpkin math (weight, circumference, longitude/latitude lines, estimating seeds), problem solving
- **Integrated Subject Areas:** nutrition, body systems, food chain, plants, rocks, senses, prairie animals, customs, Native American games, Lewis and Clark, landforms, Prairie Indians, dissecting owl pellets

December: Communities at Christmas

- **Literature:** Christmas Novels—Student Choice
- **Language Arts Focus:** Christmas book project, oral reporting, narrative writing, story elements, plot, cursive handwriting, main idea, details, public speaking, commas
- **Math Focus:** decimals, money, checkbooks, budgets, probability
- **Integrated Subject Areas:** gingerbread houses, nutrition

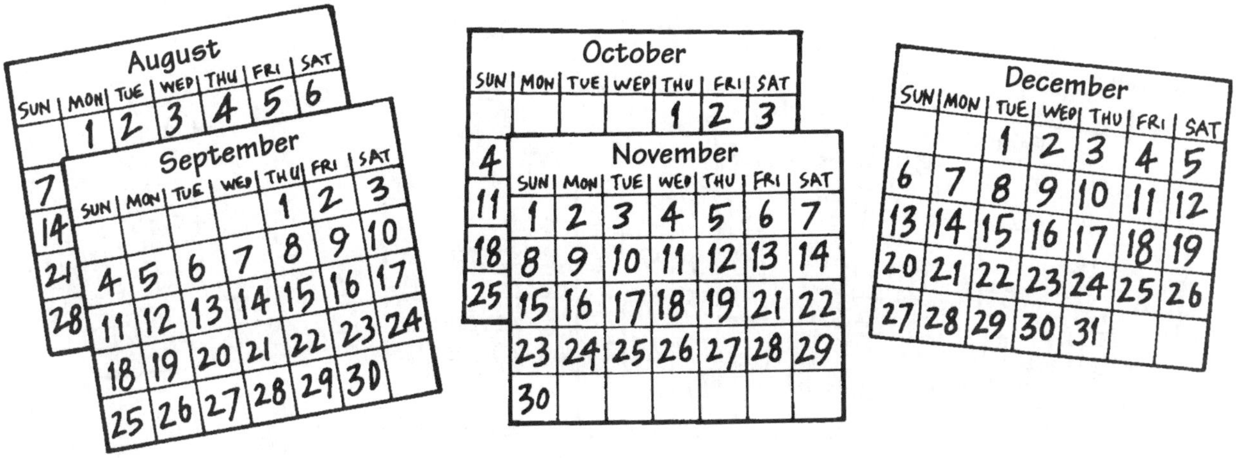

Sample Year-Long Theme: Year 3, Communities *(cont.)*

January: Cool Weather Communities

- **Literature:** *Stone Fox* by John Reynolds Gardiner
- **Language Arts Focus:** computer publishing, characters, sequence, comparing books and movies, outlines, pronouns, cause and effect, synonyms/antonyms, subject/verb agreement, complete sentences, punctuation
- **Math Focus:** measurement, money and economics, ordinals, problem solving, tables and charts
- **Integrated Subject Areas:** common sense, feelings, body systems, change, maturity, responsibility, Wyoming, Shoshone and Arapaho tribes, harmonicas, potatoes

February/March: Communities in Other Countries

- **Literature:** *Number the Stars* by Lois Lowry
- **Language Arts Focus:** adverbs, "too," possessive, contractions, fact vs. fiction, Hans Christian Andersen tales, fairy tale book report, historical fiction, informative articles, dictionary skills, capitalization, author's purpose, paragraphs
- **Math Focus:** geometry, foreign monetary units, checkbooks
- **Integrated Subject Areas:** astronomy, diet and nutrition, behavior, monarchy, Europe, World War II, solar system, cutting paper dolls, Star of David, Nazi occupation, mapping skills

April/May: Immigrant Communities

- **Literature:** *In the Year of the Boar and Jackie Robinson* by Bette Bao Lord
- **Language Arts Focus:** prefixes and suffixes, rhyming couplets, similes, Chinese characters, vocabulary, syllables, independent studies, reference materials, biographies, discussion
- **Math Focus:** abacus, averaging with baseball cards, numeration, patterns
- **Integrated Subject Areas:** origami, Chinese customs, China mapping, immigration

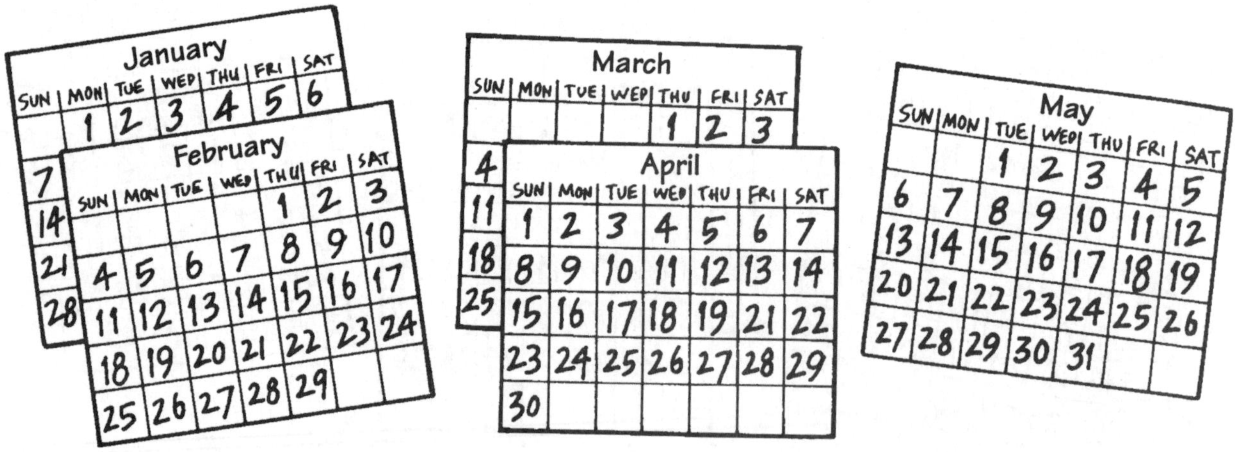

The Midnight Fox Unit Web

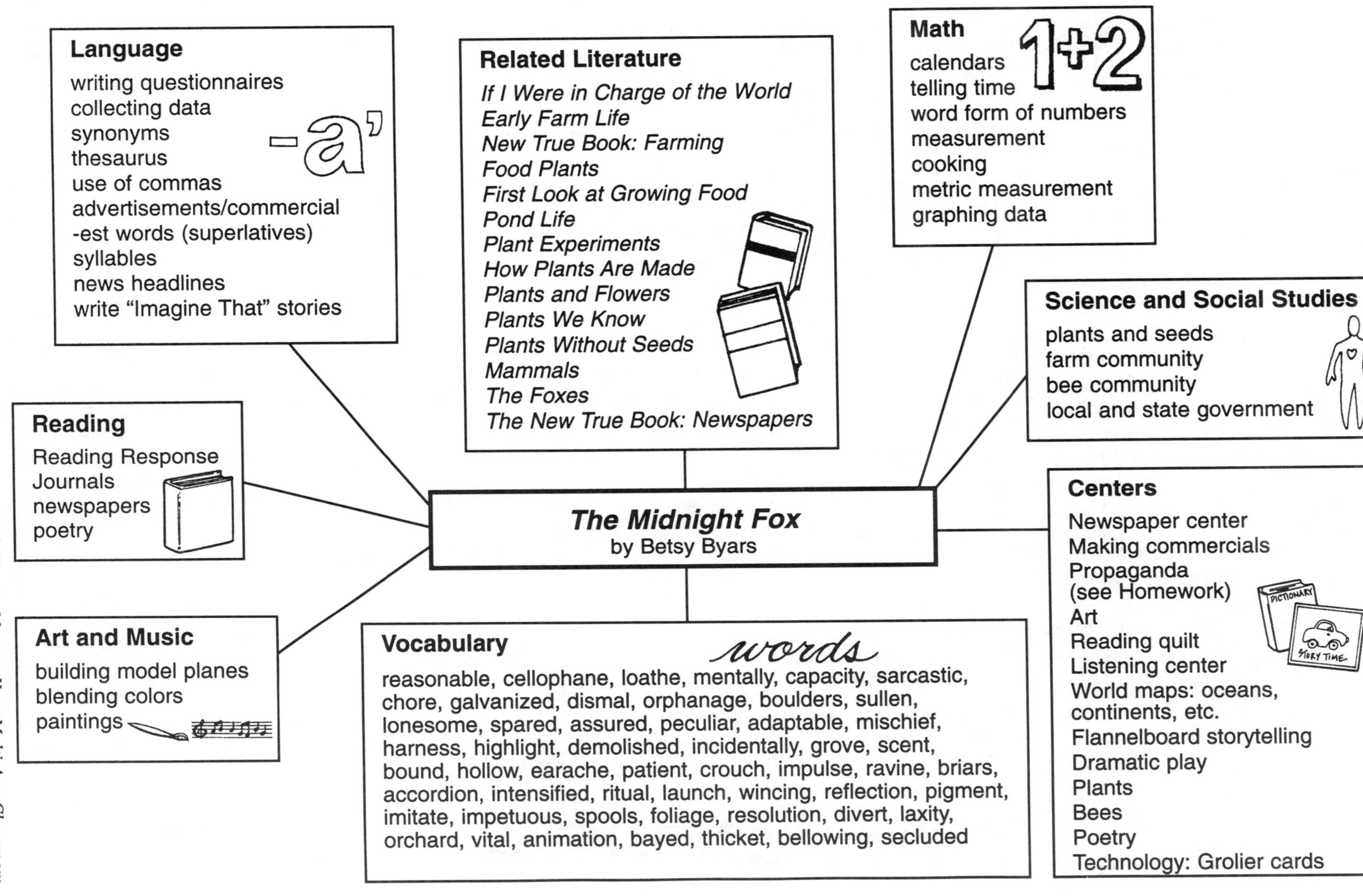

Naya Nuki Unit Web

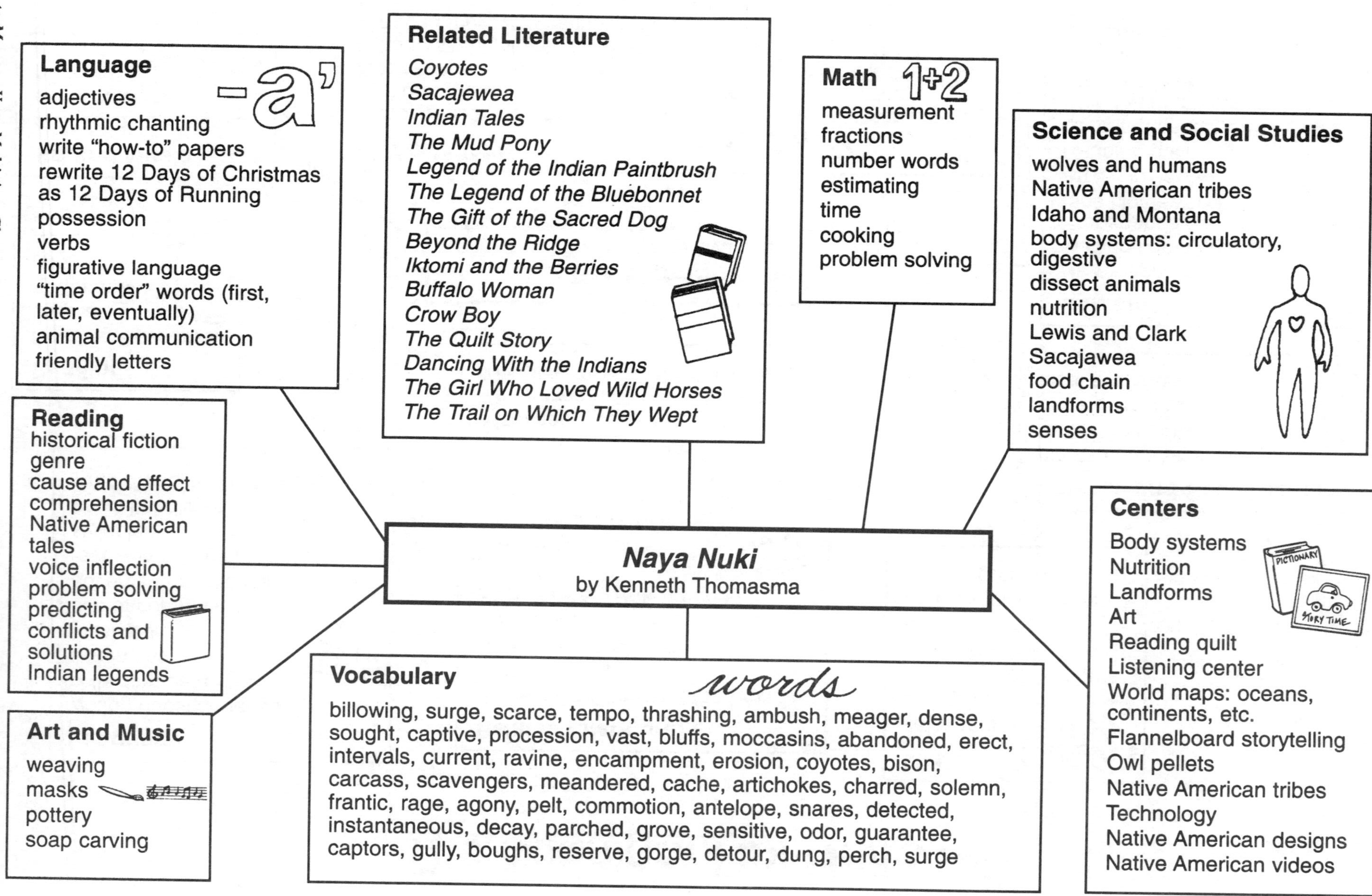

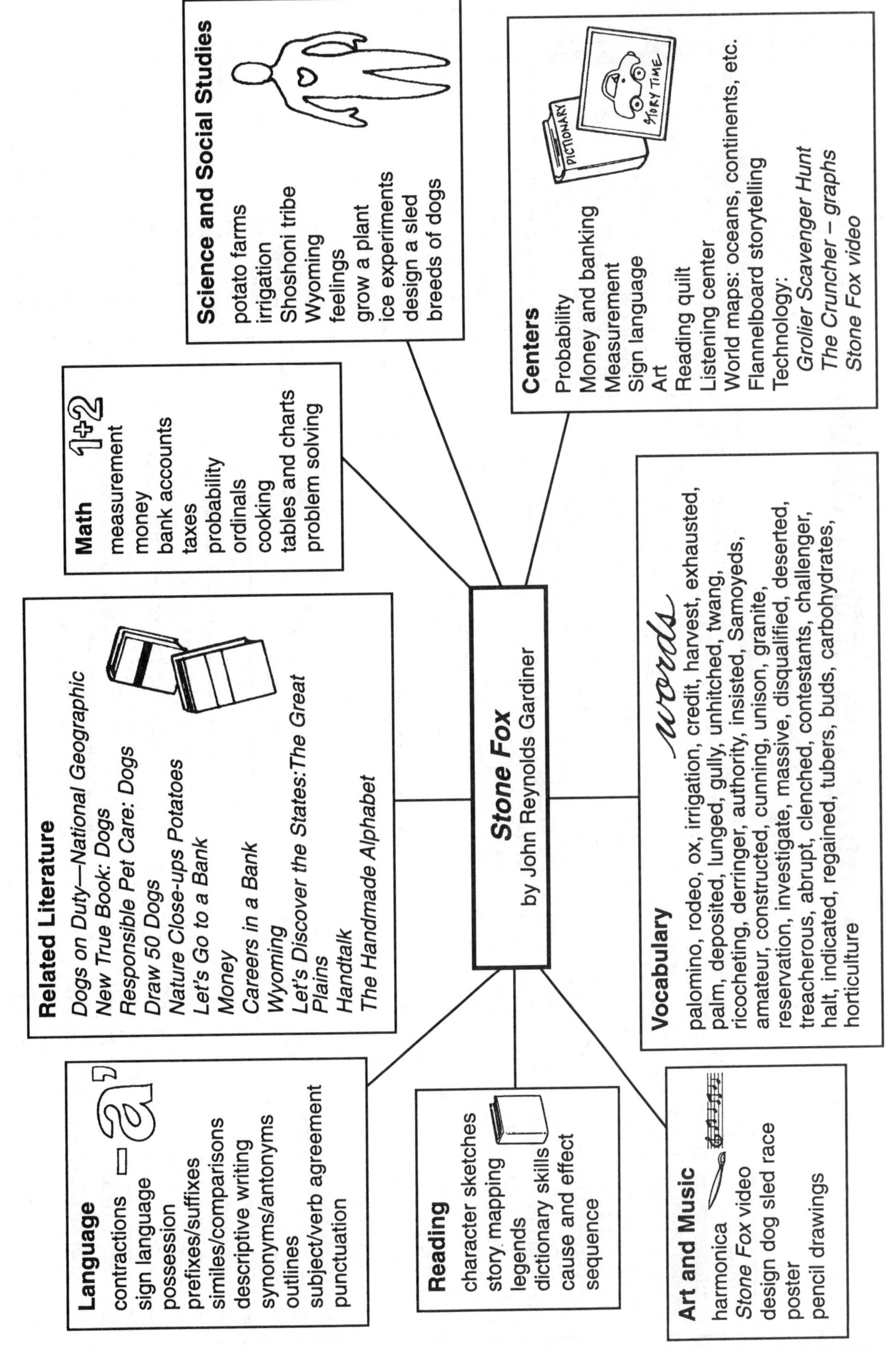
Stone Fox Unit Web
Stone Fox
by John Reynolds Gardiner
Related Literature
Dogs on Duty—National Geographic
New True Book: Dogs
Responsible Pet Care: Dogs
Draw 50 Dogs
Nature Close-ups Potatoes
Let's Go to a Bank
Money
Careers in a Bank
Wyoming
Let's Discover the States: The Great Plains
Handtalk
The Handmade Alphabet
Math
1+2
measurement
money
bank accounts
taxes
probability
ordinals
cooking
tables and charts
problem solving
Science and Social Studies
potato farms
irrigation
Shoshoni tribe
Wyoming
feelings
grow a plant
ice experiments
design a sled
breeds of dogs
Centers
Probability
Money and banking
Measurement
Sign language
Art
Reading quilt
Listening center
World maps: oceans, continents, etc.
Flannelboard storytelling
Technology:
Grolier Scavenger Hunt
The Cruncher – graphs
Stone Fox video
DICTIONARY
STORY TIME
Vocabulary
words
palomino, rodeo, ox, irrigation, credit, harvest, exhausted, palm, deposited, lunged, gully, unhitched, twang, ricocheting, derringer, authority, insisted, Samoyeds, amateur, constructed, cunning, unison, granite, reservation, investigate, massive, disqualified, deserted, treacherous, abrupt, clenched, contestants, challenger, halt, indicated, regained, tubers, buds, carbohydrates, horticulture
Language
contractions
sign language
possession
prefixes/suffixes
similes/comparisons
descriptive writing
synonyms/antonyms
outlines
subject/verb agreement
punctuation
Reading
character sketches
story mapping
legends
dictionary skills
cause and effect
sequence
Art and Music
harmonica
Stone Fox video
design dog sled race
poster
pencil drawings

Number the Stars Unit Web

Number the Stars
by Lois Lowry

Language
figurative language
capitalization
etymology of words
design a secret code
German language
role play/dramatics
adverbs
contractions/possession
"too"

Related Literature
Stepping on the Cracks
When Hitler Stole Pink Rabbit
The Lily Cupboard
Sheltering Rebecca
The Diary of Anne Frank
Let's Visit Denmark
The Second World War
The House of Sixty Fathers
As the Waltz Was Ending
The Upstairs Room
The Children We Remember
Rescue: The Story of How Gentiles Saved Jews in the Holocaust
Other books by Lois Lowry

Math
Geometry: Star of David
Roman numerals
calculators
foreign money

Science and Social Studies
map of Europe during WWII
occupied countries
Denmark
Europe: bodies of water and landforms
bravery, friendship
Science Experiments with chemicals
WWII history
The United Nations
peace
astronomy
Holocaust/Nazis

Reading
elements of fiction
Newbery Awards
Hans Christian Andersen's Tales
poetry
Bill of Rights
fact vs. fiction
author's purpose
fairytale book report
informative articles

Centers
Astronomy
Pattern blocks/problem solving
Science experiments
Art
Reading quilt
Listening center
World maps: oceans, continents, etc.
Flannelboard storytelling
Technology:
Grolier Scavenger Hunt
Planets LaserDisc
Design an Astronomy Book Page
Computer Graphics

Vocabulary
chapters 1–4: lanky, Nazi, sabotage, kroner, rabbi, Halte, occupation, rationed, swastika, synagogue
chapters 5–8: Star of David, tentatively, relocate, specter, pose, exasperation, hazy, military arrest, imprinted
chapters 9–12: urgency, typhus, unfamiliar, mourning, staccato, exhausted
chapters 13–15: stricken, latticed, contempt, sprawling, donned, visible, saliva, tantalize
chapters 16–17: warily, courageous, balcony, deprivation, permeated, concealed, anthem, executed, heroine, cocaine

Art and Music
Sound of Music songs
collage
cut paper dolls

In The Year of the Boar and Jackie Robinson Unit Web

In the Year of the Boar and Jackie Robinson
by Bette Bao Lord

Language
- prefixes and suffixes
- rhyming couplets
- similes
- Chinese characters
- oral speech
- proper nouns
- "too" "to" "two"
- vocabulary bee
- discussion

Related Literature
- *Sadako and the Thousand Paper Cranes*
- *Sports Illustrated for Kids*
- *Jackie Robinson*
- *Teammates*
- *Eyes of the Dragon*
- *Grandfather Tang's Story*
- *Cricket's Tangrams*
- *Immigrants*
- *Tikki Tikki Tembo*
- *Molly's Pilgrim*
- *Count Your Way Through China*
- *Lion Dancer*
- *The Story About Ping*

Math
- abacus
- calculations
- averaging and statistics
- baseball cards
- tangrams

Science and Social Studies
- China: map skills
- Chinese customs
- 1945 in America
- immigration
- U.S. citizenship
- inventions
- baseball/sports

Reading
- biography book report
- reference materials

Art and Music
- origami
- paper lanterns
- kaleidoscope
- cello
- scale
- sing "Happy Birthday" in Chinese
- "The Star Spangled Banner"
- chamber music
- make an abacus

Vocabulary

chapter 1: Confucian, patriarch, matriarch, dictums, harmony, irate, Buddha, abacus, squandered, threshold, generation, ebony, exiled, nurture, decreed, omen, festooned, embroidered, sequins, delicacies, celestial, feuding, melodious, ancestral

chapter 2: writhed, immigration, customs, torrential, fret, unlacquered, queried, skeptical, emphatic

chapter 3: ambassador

chapter 4: delicatessen, elaborated, stanza, forlorn, summon, scale, fluently, sapphire, sashay

chapter 5: reverent, intimidated, interrogate, ritual, pauper, desolate, excluded, meticulous

Centers
- Art
- Reading quilt
- Listening center
- World maps: oceans, continents, etc.
- Flannelboard storytelling
- Baseball—rules, history, famous players
- Immigration
- Technology: *Grolier Scavenger Hunt*

Sample Year-Long Skeleton

This form may be used by teachers to outline the main curriculum focus areas for Literature, Math, Social Studies, and Science for each week of the year. Unnecessary weeks may be crossed out, and dates can be added on the month line.

	WEEK #1	WEEK #2	WEEK #3	WEEK #4	WEEK #5
				22nd - 26th	29th - Sept. 2nd
Unit				The Midnight Fox	TMF
Math				Graphs: Computation	Graphs: Comp.
SS/S				Plants + Seeds	Plants + Seeds
	5th 9th	12th 16th	19th - 23rd	26th - 30th	
Unit	TMF	TM	{ Finish up! }	Naya Nuki	
Math				Fractions	
SS/S				Wolves + Native Americans	
	3rd - 7th	10th - 14th	17th - 21st	24th - 28th	
Unit	Naya Nuki	Naya Nuki	Naya Nuki	Naya Nuki	
Math					
SS/S					
	1st - 4th	7th - 11th	14th 18th	21st - 25th	
Unit	Naya Nuki	Naya Nuki	{ Finish up! }		28 - Dec. 2
Math					
SS/S				Thanksgiving	
		5th - 9th	12th 16th		
Unit	Christmas Novels	Christmas Novels	Christmas Novels	Christmas Break	
Math	Decimals / $				
SS/S	Christmas Customs				
	2nd - 6th	9th - 13th	16th - 20th	23rd - 27th	30th - Feb. 3rd
Unit	Stone Fox	Stone Fox	Stone Fox	Stone Fox	Stone Fox
Math					
SS/S					
		6th - 10th	13th - 17th	20th - 24th	
Unit	{ Finish Up! }	Number the Stars	Number the Stars	NtS	
Math		Geometry / $			
SS/S		Astronomy / Mapping			
	Feb. 27th - Mar. 3rd	6th - 10th	13th - 17th	20th - 24th	27th - 31st
Unit	Number the Stars	Number the Stars	Number the Stars	TCAPS	Spring Break
Math					
SS/S					
	3rd - 7th	10th - 14th	17th - 21st	24th - 28th	
Unit	Free Unit	In the Year of the Boar	In the Year...	In the Year...	
Math		Numeration / Patterns			
SS/S					
	1st - 5th	8th - 12th	15th - 19th	22 - 26th	29th - June 2nd
Unit	In the Year...	In the Year ...	In the Year...	In the Year	Free
Math					
SS/S					

Year–Long Skeleton Form

	WEEK #1	WEEK #2	WEEK #3	WEEK #4	WEEK #5
Unit					
Math					
SS/S					
Unit					
Math					
SS/S					
Unit					
Math					
SS/S					
Unit					
Math					
SS/S					
Unit					
Math					
SS/S					
Unit					
Math					
SS/S					
Unit					
Math					
SS/S					
Unit					
Math					
SS/S					
Unit					
Math					
SS/S					
Unit					
Math					
SS/S					

Sample Thematic Unit Checklist

This checklist tracks a student's progress through the basic assignments for a thematic unit. A form should be developed by team members to list activities for each unit you develop for your pod. Children learn responsibity for their work by maintaining this list themselves. The sheet may be taped to each child's desk or stapled inside a pocket folder where papers can be stored with the checklist. After the unit, the folder may become part of the student's portfolio.

Name: ________________________________ Date: ____________________

Number the Stars Unit Checklist

________ Read Social Studies pages 507–516
________ Reading Quilt
________ Maps Response
________ Grolier Task Card
________ Europe Map Handout
________ Language Arts Assignments _____ , _____ , _____ , _____ , _____ , _____ .
________ Writing Choice
________ Computer Printout: Rough Draft of a Book
________ Make a Book
________ Hans Christian Andersen Matrix Participation
________ Reading Responses (Chapters 1–2, 3–4, 5–6, 7–8, 9–10, 11–12, 13–14, 15–16, 17–Finish)
________ Math—Cooking
________ Math—Buying Items
________ Money Center
________ Star of David Geometry
________ Math Folder Assignments _____ , _____ , _____ , _____ , _____ , _____ .
________ Teach Parent a Math Game (e.g. Pig Out, Pattern Blocks)
________ Art: Cut Paper Dolls
________ Vocabulary
________ Ring of Words
________ Fact or Fiction Chart
________ Independent Study
________ Science Experiments _____ , _____ , _____ , _____ , _____ , _____ .
________ Other Center
________ Astronomy Book Page
________ Fairy Tale Book Report
________ Other Activity ____________________________
________ Other Activity ____________________________

Skills Checklists

Parents are often concerned that students in a Multi-Age class are not held accountable to state mandated objectives. They want to know how their children are progressing as compared to third, fourth, or fifth graders in traditional classrooms.

The Language Arts and Math Skills Checklists on the following pages provide lists of skills appropriate for students completing grades 3 through 5. These lists can be altered to conform to your School District Grade Level Standards.

Appropriate entries should include the date and comments, such as "counts by 2's, 5's, 10's; recalls multiplication by 2, 3, 4, 5; writes in fragments; can relate the main idea of the story."

Language Arts Skills Checklist

Name: ________________________________ Date and Comments:

FOCUS—Mechanics			
Writes legibly in cursive style.			
Uses manuscript skills for labeling, graphing, and identifying.			
Recognizes complete sentences in spoken and written language.			
Writes complete sentences using correct capitalization and punctuation.			
Capitization of titles, addresses, initials and dates.			
Uses correct ending punctuation.			
Uses commas in friendly letters, words in a series, dates, addresses, and quotes.			
Uses commas in introductory expressions and following a direct address.			
Speaks with inflection, pauses, and necessary intonation to express punctuation and give meaning to sentences.			
FOCUS—Language Usage: Parts of Speech			
nouns (common/proper, singular/plural)			
conjugates regular verbs.			
verb tense (present past, and future)			
linking and auxiliary verbs			
pronouns (case usage)			
possessive pronouns			
adjectives			
adverbs			
articles			

Language Arts Checklist *(cont.)*

Name: ______________________________ Date and Comments:

FOCUS—Sentence and Paragraph Structure			
Writes in complete sentences.			
Classifies sentences according to type (simple, compound, declarative, interrogative).			
Distinguishes between complete and incomplete sentences.			
Identifies subject and predicate (simple and compound, simple and complete).			
Subject/predicate agreement			
Forms compound sentences.			
Writes a paragraph with at least 3–5 sentences in logical order.			
Identifies inappropriate sentences in a paragraph.			
Identifies parts of a letter.			
Addresses an envelope.			
Speaks descriptively in discussion and reports.			
Develops a simple outline for pre-writing.			
Writes brief reports using notes and pertinent data.			
Proofreads for errors.			
Makes a neat final copy after proofreading.			
FOCUS–Spelling and Reading Techniques			
Spells common words in isolation or sentence dictation.			
Recognizes basic sight words.			
Arranges words in alphabetical order.			
Identifies and forms compound words.			
Recognizes correctly spelled words using sound/symbol relationships. (consonant blends, long and short vowel, diagraphs and dipthongs)			
Uses base words with suffixes and prefixes.			
Recognizes syllable patterns.			
Correctly spells contractions.			
Correctly spells possessives.			
Correctly spells plural nouns.			
Identifies stressed and unstressed syllables.			
Identifies homonyms and rhyming words.			
Identifies synonyms, given the context of sentence or a short paragraph.			
Writes abbreviations.			
Unlocks the meanings of words through use of:			
a. base words, prefixes, and suffixes.			
b. contextual clues.			
c. syllabication rules.			
Identifies silent consonants in words.			
Uses an appropriate written and oral vocabulary for grade level.			

Language Arts Skills Checklist

Name: ______________________________ Date and Comments:

FOCUS—Reading/Literary Skills			
Sequences a story in detail from memory.			
Reads selected material to:			
a. Predict events and outcomes.			
b. Identify who, what, when, why, and where.			
c. Identify cause and effect relationships.			
d. Identify author's purpose.			
e. Identify main idea of a selection.			
f. Identify story details.			
g. Sequence events from a selection.			
h. Distinguish fact from opinion.			
i. Distinguish reality from fantasy.			
j. Distinguish fiction and nonfiction.			
k. Recognize conflicts and solutions.			
l. Recognize colloquialisms.			
m. Identify and describe characters.			
n. Compare and contrast items.			
Uses context clues to formulate ideas.			
Reads for pleasure.			
Follows directions in emergency situations.			
Follows oral and written directions.			
Identifies the theme or central message of a selection.			
Identifies figurative language, similes, metaphors, and dialects.			
Recognizes time and place relationship (setting).			
Recognizes the following types of literature:			
a. autobiography			
b. biography			
c. folk and fairy tales			
d. historical fiction			
e. informative articles			
f. myths and legends			
FOCUS—Reference Study			
Uses the dictionary as a guide for alphabetizing, finding definitions, spelling, syllabication, and pronunciation.			
Selects and uses appropriate reference material (dictionary, encyclopedia, thesaurus)			
Identifies and uses parts of books: Table of Contents, Title Page, Index, Glossary.			
Interprets graphs, charts, tables, maps, and diagrams.			
Uses a telephone directory.			
Uses guide words to locate words in a dictionary.			
FOCUS—Writing			
Writes descriptively about selected topics.			
Writes a narrative.			
Writes friendly letters and business letters.			

Math Skills Checklist

Name: ______________________________ Date and Comments:

FOCUS—NUMERATION: The student will identify numbers, factors, multiples, and number values.			
Recognize and continue number patterns.			
Read and write numerals through 9,999,999.			
Identify word names for numbers through 9,999,999.			
Identify place value up to 7 digit numerals.			
Identify numbers in expanded form through 9,999,999.			
Identify even and odd numbers.			
Recognize, read, and write Roman numerals up to 1,000. (I, V, X, L, C, D, M)			
Recognize prime numbers less than 20.			
Identify ordinals to twentieth.			
Round 4 and 5 digit numerals up to 1,000.			
Order and compare numbers to 9,999,999.			
Identify the common factors of two whole numbers, each of which is less than 100.			
Identify the Greatest Common Factor of two whole numbers, each of which is less than 100.			
Identify the common multiples of two whole numbers.			
Identify the least common multiple of two whole numbers.			
Perform operations based on the use of parentheses (distributive property.)			
Write the word name for a decimal number to thousandth.			
Round decimal numbers to the nearest whole number or tenth.			
Compare the number of objects in two sets.			
Demonstrate knowledge and understanding of grade level mathematical terms. Divisor, Dividend, Addend, Sum, Subtrahend, Factor, Quotient, Remainder, Product, Multiplicand, Multiplier.			
FOCUS—WHOLE NUMBER/INTEGER OPERATIONS: The student will compute using whole numbers.			
Solve addition, subtraction, multiplication, and division problems involving monetary units.			
Count back change in bills and coins when bills are used for payment.			
Solve addition, subtraction, multiplication, and division problems involving monetary units.			
Determine money value from a collection of coins and bills to $1,000.00.			

Math Skills Checklist *(cont.)*

Name: ______________________________ Date and Comments:

Add multi-digit numbers up to 5 addends.			
Subtract multi-digit numbers up to 5 addends.			
Recall from memory multiplication and division facts through 12.			
Multiply 2 and 3 digit numbers without a zero.			
Divide a 2 digit number by a 2 digit number with or without a remainder.			
Divide a 3 digit number by a 1 or 2 digit number with or without a remainder.			
Determine probability.			
Solve one and two step word problems involving any combination of basic operations on whole numbers.			
Read simple word problems, including those with whole numbers, fractions, or decimals, and use the appropriate operation to calculate the answer.			
FOCUS—FRACTIONS: The student will identify and compare fractions with like and unlike denominators.			
Read and interpret a picture graph with partial figures.			
Identify the numerator and denominator of a fraction.			
Read simple word problem, including those with whole numbers, fractions, or decimals, and use the appropriate operation to calculate the answer.			
Reduce fractions to lowest terms using the Greatest Common Factor.			
Compare fractions having unlike denominators by finding the common denominator.			
Identify a mixed number and an improper fraction.			
Change improper fractions to mixed numbers and vice versa, reducing fractions to lowest terms.			
Add fractions having like denominators with and without regrouping.			
Subtract fractions having like denominators with and without regrouping.			
Add fractions having unlike denominators without regrouping.			

Math Skills Checklist *(cont.)*

Name: ______________________________ Date and Comments:

Rename mixed fractional numbers.			
Add and subtract mixed numbers.			
Solve simple word problem, including those with whole numbers, fractions, or decimals, using the appropriate operation to calculate the answer.			
FOCUS—DECIMALS: Identify decimal numbers to thousandths.			
Identify decimal place value to thousandths.			
Write the word name for a decimal number to thousandth.			
Determine the decimal equivalent of a fraction with a denominator of 10 or 100.			
Identify the greater or lesser of two decimal numbers to thousandths.			
Add decimal numbers including mixed numbers to thousandths.			
Subtract decimal numbers including mixed numbers to thousandths.			
Round decimal numbers to the nearest whole number or tenth.			
Add and subtract using decimals, money, and cent symbols.			
FOCUS—GRAPHS: Use information from graphs, tables, and charts to answer questions.			
Locate points on a grid.			
FOCUS—MEASUREMENT: Identify standard temperatures on Celsius and Fahrenheit thermometers.			
Identify metric and customary relationships (m/cm, kg/g, km/m, lb/oz, ft/in yd/ft)			
Measure to the nearest mm or 1/4 - inch.			
FOCUS—TIME: Identify time relationships and convert units of time.			
Indicate time to the nearest minute on a standard clock.			
FOCUS—GEOMETRY: Identify points, lines, rays, cube, cone, sphere, cylinder, obtuse angles, acute angles, line segments, right angles, and vertice.			
Find the perimeter and area of a polygon.			
Label the diameter, circumference, radius and center of a circle.			

Individual Math Folders

Assignment Scope and Sequence

This continuous math development sequence provides a logical progression of math skills. Individual math folders focus primarily on addition, subtraction, multiplication, and division.

1. Simple addition in families
2. Place Value: 1's, 10's, 100's
3. Addition with regrouping
4. Addition with money and decimals
5. Addition of four or five digits
6. Addition of columns
7. Simple subtraction in families
8. Subtraction with regrouping
9. Subtraction with zero
10. Subtraction with money and decimals
11. Subtraction of four or five digits
12. Demonstrates addition/subtraction using manipulatives
13. Uses correct terminolgy for parts of an addition or subtraction problem
14. Multiplication: Student is able to demonstrate multiplication using manipulatives, pictures, addition.
15. Use correct terminolgy to label the parts of a problem and other multiplication terms.
16. One digit multiplication
17. One digit x two digits
18. One digit x two digits with regrouping
19. Identifies multiples and factors
20. Multiply 2 digits x 2 digits using grid multiplication.
21. Multiples of 10
22. Multiplying by multiples of 10
23. Multiplying by harder multiples of 10 (eg. 20, 30, 200 . . .)
24. Expanded multiplication—Separate to multiply, then regroup.

e.g.				
	45	45	45	45
	x 62	x2	x60	x62
		90	2,700	90
				2,700
				2,790

25. Multiplying 2-digit x 3-digit numbers
26. Multiplies with money and decimals.
27. Division: Student is able to demonstrate division using manipulatives, illustrations, repeated subtraction.
28. Student is able to label the parts of a division problem.
29. Writes a division problem as a fraction, using division house, or the division sign.
30. Divides using repeated subtraction.
31. Divides a one-digit divisor with no remainder; check with multiplication.
32. Divides a one-digit divisor with remainder; check with multiplication.
33. Division: calculator checking
34. Division: Rounding to the nearest ten, hundred, thousand
35. Division: Two-digit divisor as a multiple of ten
36. Averaging Numbers
37. Averages project
38. Reads and writes decimals
39. Rounds off decimals
40. Division with decimals and money

Classroom
Management

Discipline in the Multi-Age Classroom

As in any classroom, discipline in the Multi-Age program is essential to the academic progress and security of each student. Even though a student ultimately chooses his or her own behavior, it is important to look past the child's actions to see the underlying cause. Often the behavior can be linked to the child seeking attention, revenge, power, or avoiding failure. Rudolf Dreikurs, a prominent psychiatrist, classified children's misbehavior into these four broad categories. In addition to this consideration, a teacher may evaluate classroom practices which can be encouraging the misbehavior. A few things to look for include inconsistency, inactivity, discrimination, a lack of humor, meaningless or boring instruction, or a lack of support. Finally, remember that students are human and may make mistakes. They need to feel significant and encouraged. Some suggestions for supporting a child include stressing the child's good qualities or successful experiences, asking for the child's thoughts about the misbehavior, and deciding on a solution together.

Helpful Tips

1. Model the behaviors that you expect from your students.
2. Modify assignments for students by planning developmentally appropriate activities which give attention to a child's learning style.
3. Try not to take student behaviors personally. Remain calm, fair, and firm when disciplining.
4. Establish a "Time Out" area at the beginning of the year.
5. Provide children with opportunities to make choices.
6. Give students an opportunity to be helpers and to be responsible.
7. Allow children a chance to share special interests during class.
8. Teach children how to appropriately express their feelings and needs and to interact with others.
9. Seat needy children near you and away from other potentially disrupting or distracting children.
10. Play instrumental music during work times.
11. Provide encouragement so children experience success a majority of the time.
12. When you feel overwhelmed, find support.
13. Enlist assistance from other team members for a child with special needs.

Conduct Report

Students are given a conduct report chart to keep on their desks. Instruct the children when to put appropriate codes on their chart. The codes are listed in a positive manner to describe the expected behavior. It is important to use a symbol on the chart to record and encourage appropriate behaviors. Students may take the conduct report home to be signed at the end of the week and returned to the teacher.

Sample form

Name: Andrea Smith

My Conduct Report for the week of: February 2–6

Monday	☆	SC	☆							
Tuesday	☆	BR	☆	SC						
Wednesday	TA	☆	☆							
Thursday	☆	TA	SC	☆	☆	☆				
Friday	☆	☆	SC	☆						

Code: Students needs to improve these behaviors.

FD – Follow Directions
BR – Be Responsible
SC – Self Control

SR – Show Respect
TA – Talk Appropriately

☆= A star indicates appropriate behavior during the day.

Ms. Victoria Smith
Parent Signature

Name: ______________

My Conduct Report for the week of: ______________

Monday										
Tuesday										
Wednesday										
Thursday										
Friday										

Code: Students needs to improve these behaviors.

FD – Follow Directions
BR – Be Responsible
SC – Self Control

SR – Show Respect
TA – Talk Appropriately

☆= A star indicates appropriate behavior during the day.

____
Parent Signature

Multi-Age Student Behavior Report

A child should fill out this form when sent to Time Out to help him actively monitor his behavior. Later the form can be used as the teacher and student discuss the behavior. The teacher may keep the forms on file for future reference during conferences.

Multi-Age Student Behavior Report

Name: ____________________ Date: ________________

Describe what happened.____

____

____

____

____

____

____

____

At first I was feeling ____

because ____

____

I could have solved the situation better by choosing to ____________________

____

____

Now I want to ____

____

Feeling words:

- afraid
- angry
- bored
- cheated
- sad
- confused
- happy
- picked on
- ignored
- timid
- hurt
- disappointed

Sample Behavior Analysis Report

This behavior report can be a model for teachers to follow when a child is behaving inappropriately despite using all available methods to support the child. This form can be used at parent meetings as an effective tool in communicating a child's progress.

Name: Susan Martin Date: March 23

Main Goal: To help Susan be a positive and productive participant in the classroom – Multi-Age

Observations:

1. Susan is expected to pursue assignments, follow directions, recognize her citizenship obligations, and not infringe upon the rights of other.
2. Susan playfully destroys private property of others. When asked to stop she continues, spits, punches, and pokes others.
3. Susan often makes negative remarks to other students especially name calling.
4. Susan appears to disregard the numerous resources provided in attempts to stimulate learning and improve behavior.
5. Susan rarely completes work independently or logs assignments.
6. Susan rarely takes responsibility to complete assignments, even when interests are self selected and at her ability level.

Recommendation: I believe that Susan's behavior has detrimental to the learning of other students. Therefore, I recommend that we take action to improve Susan's behavior.

Behavior Analysis Report Form

Name: ______________________________ Date: ________________

Main Goal: ____

____

____

____

Observations:

1. ____
   ____
2. ____
   ____
3. ____
   ____
4. ____
   ____
5. ____
   ____
6. ____
   ____

Recommendation: ____

____

____

____

Instruction

Instructional Strategies

This list suggests a variety of teaching strategies which can be integrated into each thematic unit in a Multi-Age class. Several instructional strategies can be combined successfully.

- **Individualization/Individual Math Folders**—Each child has a separate assignment.
- **Learning Centers**—Engaging activities students may choose that are available throughout the class
- **Whole Language, Literature-based Instruction**—Integrating language skills with other subject areas
- **Individual Goal Setting and Continuous Progress Interviews**—Each child's growth is assessed individually.
- **Writing Across the Curriculum**—Writing about math, science, and social studies
- **Letter Writing/Dialogue Folders**—Students and teachers write letters to each other.
- **Cooperative Learning**—Students work cooperatively in small groups.
- **Reading Response Journals**—Students respond individually to something they have read.
- **Self-Evaluation**—Students evaluate their own progress.
- **Peer Evaluation, Peer Editing, and Peer Tutoring**—Students assist one another and mark each other's progress.
- **Student-led Parent Conferences**—Students explain and show evidence of their learning at a conference with parents and the teacher.
- **Skills Instruction**—Whole Group and Small Group—Group lessons that teach a particular skill and last approximately 15 minutes.
- **Hands-on Mathematics** (*Math Their Way* and *Math a Way of Thinking*)—Students explore math concepts and relationships by manipulating objects.
- **Independent Studies**—Students choose a topic they would like to learn about. They list what they already know, what they want to know, and resources they are going to use. A final product describing what they learned is shared.
- **The Writing Process and Writing Assessments**—Students write, revise, edit, and make a final draft.
- **Hands-on, Discovery Science, Explorations, Inquiry and Investigations**—Students conduct experiments, hypothesize, test, retest, and make conclusions.
- **Flexible Grouping**—Grouping varies and is based upon student needs.
- **Discussion Groups/Seminars**—Each student is encouraged to participate in discussing a relevant topic.
- **Drama and Shared Reading**—Students are actively engaged in storytelling.
- **Problem Solving**—Students apply skills and knowledge in new ways to solve problems.
- **Open-ended Statements**—Students give a response to conclude a thought.
- **Webbing, Outlining, Charting, Venn Diagrams**—Students organize information graphically.
- **Research**—Students use a variety of resources to locate information.
- **Technological Applications**—Students use technology for research and design.

Flexible Groupings

The teaching team should plan, discuss, and schedule whole pod grouping arrangements. If each class in the pod is planning the same activity, for instance watching a theme-related filmstrip, it may be easier to plan the activity at one time for all classes. Block scheduling may be appropriate for certain units, as well as needs grouping for math and writing.

Whole Multi-Age Pod Group

Beginning School Activity
Singing and Exercising
Pledge
Pod schedule and specific needs
Filmstrips
Integrated Videos
Current Events
Center Sharing/performance assessments
Writing assessments
Silent reading time
Guest speakers
Appropriate experiments

Whole Class Group

Appropriate group lessons
Skills instruction
Teacher reading to class
Class schedule and needs
Teacher modeling
Art instruction
Seminar (Literature Discussion Group)
Center Sharing/performance assessments
Appropriate experiments

Small Groups

Beginning School Activity
Reteaching
Similar interests sharing
Project groups
Cooperative learning
Discussion groups
Peer tutoring
Dramatic play
Centers
Reading
Math instruction
Video productions
Storytelling

Individual/One-on-One

Independent study
Conference with teacher
Reteaching
Evaluating individual skills
Responding to child's progress
Portfolio sharing
Spelling practice
Centers
Reading
Math instruction
Math facts practice
Various assessments
Computer creations and application

Teacher's Lesson Planning Sheet

Focus: Goals and Objectives for the lesson

Appropriateness for all levels:

Concrete enough?

Hands-on materials/activities:

What students will be doing during the lesson	**What the teacher will be doing during the lesson**

How will achievement of objectives be measured? When?

What is the next step for students?

Sample Schedule of a Day

This page outlines the progression of a typical day in a Multi-Age classroom. Even though the daily schedule may vary, time should be allotted for the following activities each week: math instruction, oral reading, silent reading, writing, centers, integrated subject areas. Teachers may rearrange the schedule to fit their needs.

7:45–8:15 **Preparation.** Children report to their homerooms for attendance, lunch count, and storage of personal items. BSA's (Beginning School Assignment) are completed in each child's individual folder to maximize use of time and get the students in a ready-to-work mode.

8:15 **Movement, Singing, and Chanting.** This can be teacher or student led, in homerooms, or whole group.

8:30 **Large Group.** The children and teachers come together in the largest pod room to talk about the day's schedule, announcements, and important events from life outside of school.

8:40–10:30 **Language Arts Block and Flexible Snack Time.** Includes a whole group, small group, partner, or individual reading time; language arts mini-lesson and activity; seminar, and writing time. This block usually ends with student writings sharing time.

Centers. Whenever students finish block activities, they may go to a center. Scheduling for center time depends on teacher choice, and may include several hours on selected days as needed. Center time for students is meant as an activity that is more independently motivated; however, students can choose from prepared activities. A project handed in, a demonstration, or performance assessment is expected from the child upon completion of a center.

10:30–11:45 **Math Block.** May begin with a whole group mini-lesson, followed by small group, individual, or independent activities. Students may work in individual math folders toward goals. The children learn to apply math concepts by using a variety of manipulative materials. Students work as independently as possible, with teachers moving among students asking and answering questions and teaching new ideas.

11:45 **Oral Reading to Children Before Lunch.**

12:30–1:00 **Lunch Recess.** The children have a half hour to stretch and exercise their developing muscles outside. Children often organize their own games during the recess period.

1:00–1:30 **Recreational Reading and Letter Writing Time.** Children place selected books or magazines on their desks before lunch so they are prepared to enter the room, sit down, and read silently. Soft music during this period can contribute to the quiet-time atmosphere. Teachers can make use of this time by listening to selected students read, asking questions to check interest, readability, and comprehension. Students learn that reading is an enjoyable activity, an end in itself. Selected students write a letter to their homeroom teacher in a dialogue folder. The teacher writes to each child in her homeroom once each week.

1:30–2:30 **ISA** (Integrated Subject Activities) Can include social studies, science, art, physical education, and technology activities relating to the theme.

2:30 **Cleanup.** Learning to clean up creates in children a sense of ownership in the classroom and a sense of responsibility in planning future activities. The children are also responsible for collecting their own homework, clothing and other possessions.

2:45 **Dismissal.**

Sample Beginning School Assignment (BSA) Activities

Each morning a Beginning School Activity may be written on a chalkboard for every child to work on independently. Students should write responses to the BSA's in a folder. Go over the BSA as a whole group. Choose additional BSA activities from appropriate skills and objectives in your state curriculum guide.

Day 1

Read the following directions; then draw your picture on a blank sheet of notebook paper.

1. Draw a big house.
2. Put a tree by the house.
3. Put six apples on the tree.
4. Put a boy by the house.
5. Put a brown bird on the house.
6. Put a red wagon under the tree.

Day 2

Make a September calendar. Use Roman Numerals to number each day.

Day 3

Use your September calendar to answer these questions.

1. How many weekend days (Saturdays and Sundays) are in September?
2. Add up all the days that end in 0 or 5. What is the sum?
3. Subtract the first day of the month from the last day.
4. If there were 35 days in September, what day would the 35th fall on?
5. Look at the dates for each Friday. What is a pattern you see?

Day 4

Rewrite this friendly letter with correct capitals and punctuation. Then label the five main parts of the letter. (Heading, Greeting, Body, Closing, and Signature)

september 3 1996

dear students

monday was labor day we took a picnic lunch to cades cove i took off my shoes and waded in the river then we threw a frisbee later we roasted marshmallows over a fire

your friend
mrs jones

Sample Beginning School Assignment: (BSA) Activities *(cont.)*

Day 5

Rewrite these events from (any story your class is reading) in the correct sequence.

Day 6

Arrange the words on each line in an order that clearly makes a sentence.

1. are doing how you?
2. hope you have I day a nice.
3. you your can story read?
4. has times his read three story Jim.
5. proud school I'm in doing how of are you.

Day 7

Draw a bar graph to show the following information.

The Tornadoes played a basketball game against the Rebels. Joey scored 6 points. Demarcus scored 11 points. Michael scored 16 points. Carlos scored half as many points as Michael. Steven scored 6 more points than Joey.

Day 8

Name the fewest coins needed for each amount.

1. $.19 =
2. $.35 =
3. $.52 =
4. $.83 =
5. $.21 =
6. $.64 =
7. $.98 =
8. $.46 =
9. $.77 =

Day 9

Copy each word. Then write the plural form of each word.

baby ________	play ________	movie ________	sheep ________
monkey ________	apple ________	shoe ________	beep ________
child ________	fox ________	mouse ________	house ________
party ________	penny ________	tomato ________	rodeo ________

Day 10

Copy each set of numbers. Then, write the next three numbers for each of the patterns.

4, 6, 8, 10, ________, ________, ________

65, 60, 55, ________, ________, ________

9, 12, 15, 18, ________, ________, ________

42, 36, 30, ________, ________, ________

13, 20, 27, ________, ________, ________

49, 36, 25, 16, ________, ________, ________

Songs and Chants Resources

Recordings by Rick Charette

Bubblegum

Alligator in the Elevator

I've Got Super Power

Where Do My Sneakers Go at Night?

Christmas Tree

Chickens on Vacation

A Little Peace and Quiet

An Evening With Rick Charette

Pine Point Record Company

P.O. Box 901 Windham, Maine 04062

Records and Cassette Tapes by Jack Grunsky

Imaginary Window, 1988

Children of the Morning, 1990.

Youngheart Music, P.O. Box 6017, Cypress, CA 90630-0017

1-800-444-4287

Record and Cassette Tape by Mr. Al

Bop 'Till You Drop

Melody House, Oklahoma City, OK 73114

Record by Jane Murphy

Journey Into Space, 1988

KIMBO Educational, Box 477, Long Branch, NJ 07740

Cassette Tape—*Multiplication Motivation.* Melody House (MH-C14)

Cassette Tapes by Bob Reid and Friendz

Marz Barz

Blue Bear Records (408)-662-0164

Cassette Tapes, Records, and CD's by Greg and Steven

We All Live Together Volume 1–5

Kids in Motion

Holidays and Special Times

Youngheart Music, P.O. Box 6017, Cypress, CA 90630-0017

1-800-444-4287

Records by Raffi (also available in CD's and cassette tape)

The Corner Grocery Store, 1979

Evergreen, Everblue, 1990

More Singable Songs

MCA Records, 70 Universal City Plaza, Universal City, CA 91608

Record by Vickie Noes

Teaching With the Holidays

Brentwood Kids Company, One Maryland Farms, Suite 200, Brentwood, TN 37027

Record by Ella Jenkins

You'll Sing a Song, I'll Sing a Song

Smithsonian Folkways, One Camp Street, Cambridge, MA 02140

Reading Log Form

After completing the Beginning School Activity, students will read independently, maintaining completed Reading Log Forms in their portfolio to show reading progress and book choices. Students should have a copy of this page to keep in the front cover of their BSA folders.

Name:______________________________ Teacher: ______________________

Date	Book Title and Author	Pages Read From	To	Genre	Personal Comments

Reading Quilt

Students should have a copy of the reading quilt stapled to the back cover of their BSA Folder to accompany the Reading Log Form.

As you read one of the following genres of writing, write the title of the book in the matching quilt section and color it. When you have colored the entire quilt, it will be placed on the wall beside the book shelf in our classroom.

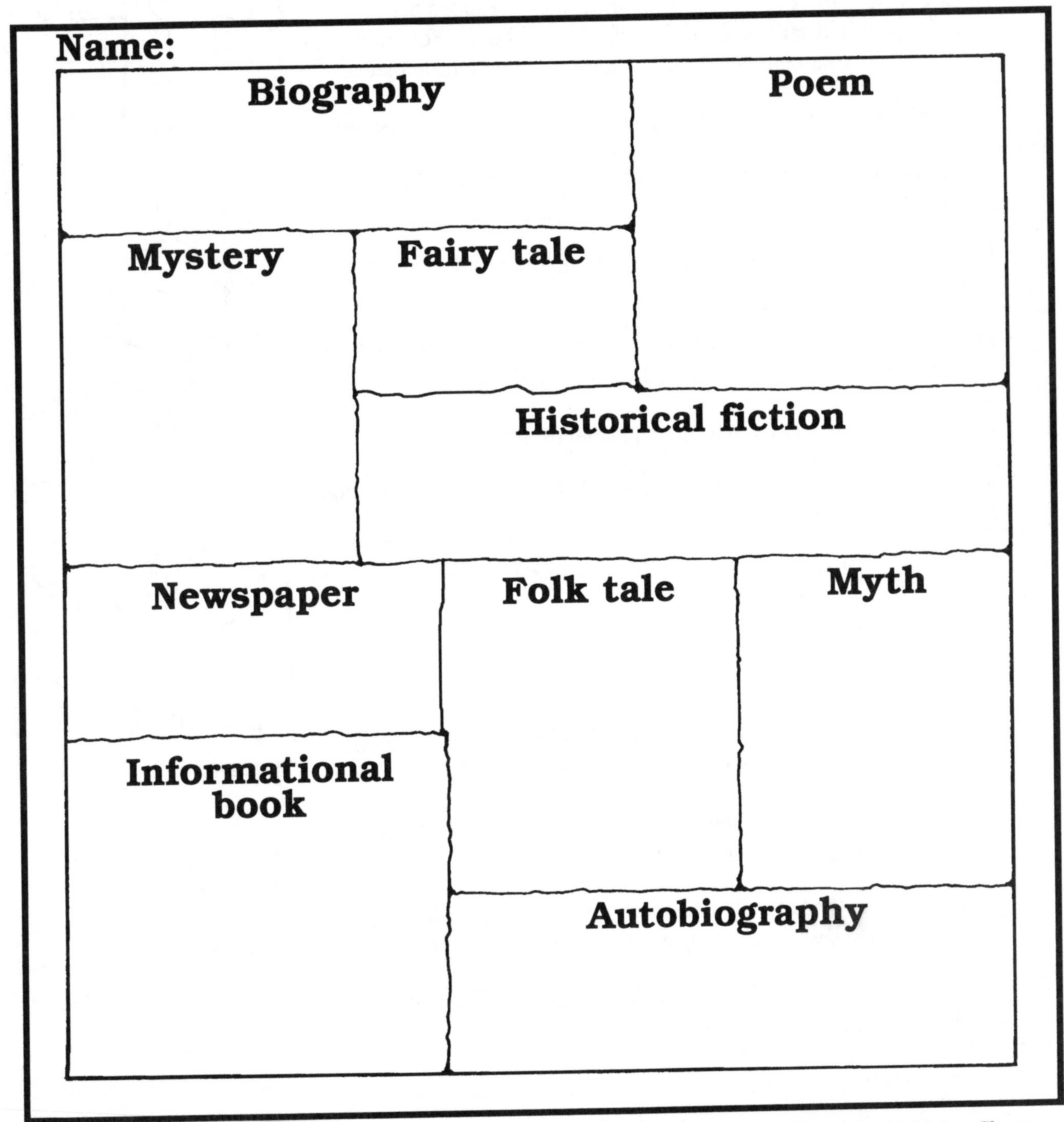

Literature Extension Activities

This list will help give you additional ideas for activities that students can do once they finish reading a book. These ideas will be helpful during the December, which is Christmas or Hannukah book choice time each year of the curriculum cycle.

- Create a one-person performance featuring yourself as the main character.
- Make a plot chart sequencing the major events from the story.

- Draw a picture of your favorite part of the story. Remember to include specific details that are described in the book. You may choose to cut your completed illustration into large puzzle pieces.
- Draw a Venn diagram comparing yourself to a character in the story.
- List each character and describe how they changed as the story progressed.
- Create a map of places mentioned in the book. Include a key and symbols.

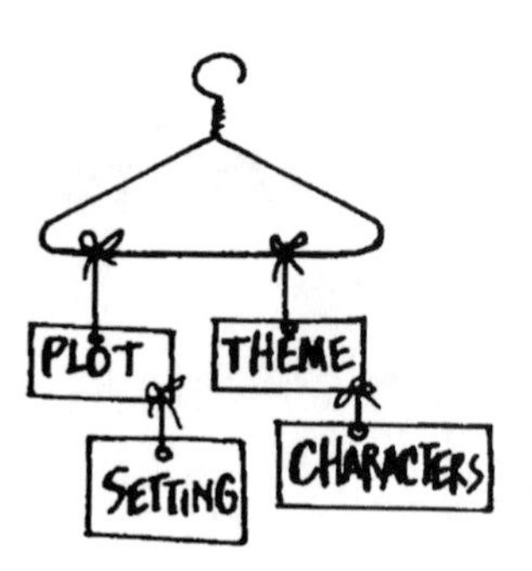

- Design character puppets, write a script for the puppets that includes details from the story, and present the show to the class.
- Draw a comic strip to show what happened in the story.
- Make a mobile on a hanger that explains the story elements: setting, plot, characters, theme.
- Create a collage of words and pictures that relate to the book.

- Create a video production of the book.
- Design a board game that relates to the book.
- Write a letter to a character in the book, giving the character advice on what to do or what he needs to consider before making decisions.
- Design a newspaper front page that relates to the story. Include lead story, cut, cut line, flag, and headline.

- Interview the author or main character of the story. Create your own questions and answers. You may ask a partner to assist you.
- Write a letter recommending the book to a friend. Give five specific reasons why you recommend the book.
- Write a sequel to the story.

Sample Reading Response Group Discussion Form

When more than one piece of literature is being used for reading groups, this form helps the teacher keep track of student responses during a group reading seminar. Codes are used to keep track of the types of comments being made.

Group: Soup Date: November 14

Meeting #_______ Name	Shared Q = Asked ?'s, P = Predicted, R = Responded, C = Made connections to life or within book	Notes
David	Didn't read. Head down. No comments. C - just a story Made up a response based on what others said	Will read ch. 3 & 4.
Jason	C - changed Schools Q	* Wants to switch groups.
Marilyn	R R-With Facts! R-Acorn Pipes R- torture	No Written Response
Ralph	C- 1st grade R-Retelling R P - Bully will get soup R-Vocabulary	* Work on complete sentences
Jess	Absent.	
Joanna	R R-Retelling ch.2 Relate to whipping C-Water Balloons C-cat to electric wire	Excellent response.
Carlene	C R Typed a response	* Playing with pen & book.

Reading Response Group Discussion Form

Group: ______________________________ Date: ______________

Meeting #______ Name	Shared Q = Asked ?'s, P = Predicted, R = Responded, C = Made connections to life or within book	Notes

Students receive a copy of this chart to place on the inside front cover of their writing folders. Each written assignment should be logged onto this page.

Name: ______________________________ Date: ______________

Teacher: ______________________________

Pieces I Have Written

Date	Title	Type of Writing	Personal Evaluation

Sample Topical Writing Approach

This organizational method can help children group their thoughts for outlining, interviewing, conducting independent studies and writing essays or reports having several paragraphs. Each child should be given at least three 3"x 5" index cards or use the topical writing approach form on the next page. Ask students to brainstorm a list of questions they have about a particular topic on a sheet of paper. Teach students not to ask questions that can be answered by "yes" or "no." From that list of questions, three good questions may be chosen for research.

On one side of an index card, draw a line down the middle of the card and have students list a question on one side of the line and the main answer on the other. This information becomes a good topic sentence. More elaborate details concerning the question should be listed on the other side of the index card. The details become the supporting sentences of the paragraph. This helps students write paragraphs that stick to the main topic and are not repetitive.

Question	Answer	More Details
1. What happened before the Revolutionary War Started?	Before the Revolutionary War England ruled America.	There was a French and Indian War. England set taxes on printed material, tea, etc. The Sons of Liberty had the Boston Tea Party.
2. What happened during the Revolutionary War?	Americans began to want their independence	The Continental Congress met in Philadelphia to plan rules for the colonies. The first battle took place at Lexington. "Shot heard round the World."
3. What happened at the end of the War and after?	Americans won the war, got their independence, and had to plan their own government.	Treaty of Paris was written ending the war. The Americans won the last battle at Yorktown.

Topical Writing Approach Form

Question	Answer	More Details

Question	Answer	More Details

Question	Answer	More Details

Writing Prompts

Everyone has had the experience of staring at a blank piece of paper and not knowing where to begin a writing assignment. The following prompts focus on stimulating a student's thoughts for descriptive writing. Successful descriptions convey a sensory experience so vivid that the reader is able to share the writer's experience of the person, place, or thing being described. Additional types of writing include narratives (discussing a connected sequence of events), expository writing (explaining or describing a process in order), and persuasion (convincing the reader through a logical argument).

Giving a prompt to students to write on may follow whole group brainstorming on the general topic. Students should be taught ways to organize their thoughts, such as webbing or outlining, each time they brainstorm for a writing prompt.

Among other appropriate prompts are the 5 W's: Who, What, Where, When, and Why?

1. Describe a typical lunchtime at your school. Tell what you hear, see, smell, touch, and taste during a typical lunchtime. Describe it so that someone who has never eaten at your school can understand it.

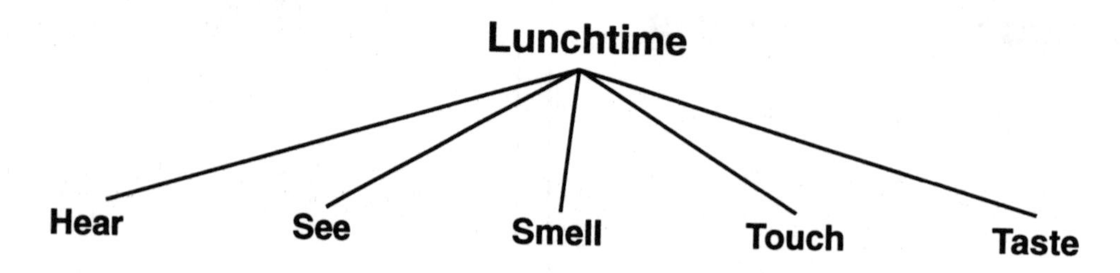

2. It is a sunny, summer day. You get to plan the schedule of your day. Describe what you will do, see, hear, smell, touch, and taste throughout the day.
3. Imagine you own a magic carpet that can take you anywhere you choose. Tell what you hear, see, smell, touch, and taste during one of your adventures on the magic carpet.
4. Imagine you are walking outside on a rainy day. Describe what you might hear, see, smell, and touch.
5. Imagine you are at a pet store and can take home any animal you choose. Write a story about your first day with your new pet.
6. Think about your favorite place to visit. Describe this place for your teacher. What do you see, hear, smell, touch, and taste there?
7. Tell about a favorite story you have read, heard, or seen on television or at the movies. Include interesting details about characters, places, events, and ideas.
8. Describe one of your favorite holidays. Describe what you hear, see, smell, touch, and taste on this day.
9. Describe your ultimate idea of a day off from school. What would you do, see, hear, smell, touch, and taste?

Editing Checklists

Students are expected to assess themselves and their peers so they can see first hand why writing must make sense and be clearly organized. As editors, they learn to understand and appreciate the process of proofreading and revising. Two checklists are offered to accommodate different ability levels.

Editing Checklist #1

Instructions: Read your story after you finish writing it to make sure you have met the following criteria. If you find that you have overlooked something, rewrite your story, then check the box. After you have checked it, ask a friend to edit it again.

Date ____________________ Title ______________________________________

Author ____________________________ Editor__________________________

Author	Editor	Criteria
☐	☐	The story has a beginning, a middle, and an end.
☐	☐	The story makes sense.
☐	☐	Each sentence begins with a capital letter.
☐	☐	Proper nouns begin with a capital letter.
☐	☐	Each sentence ends with punctuation.

Editing Checklist #2

Instructions: Read your work carefully to make sure that you have met the following criteria. Make changes if necessary, then ask another person to edit your work.

Date ____________________ Title ______________________________________

Author ____________________________ Editor__________________________

_______ 1. I read my story to a friend to see if it makes sense.

_______ 2. I deleted extra words that I don't need.

_______ 3. I capitalized "I," all names, and the beginning of each sentence.

_______ 4. I underlined words that may be misspelled.

_______ 5. I replaced weak words with specific words.

_______ 6. I indented each paragraph.

_______ 7. I checked for correct punctuation. (. ? ! , " " ')

Error Tally Sheet

Each student receives a copy of this form to put in the back cover of the writing folder. Students are taught how to record the frequency of their writing errors. Only the rules appropriate for the child to know are marked so this form responds to individual learner needs.

Name: ______________________

GRAMMAR	MECHANICS	PUNCTUATION	EXACTNESS	SPELLING
Verbs Subjects Parts of Speech Sentences Fragments Combining Sentences	Right Word Subject/Verb Agreement Proofreading Form Capitals	Quotation Marks Commas Punctuation Marks	Wordiness Mature Vocabulary Fresh Expressions Paragraph Form Variety	Rules Suffixes Hyphens a/an Phonics Misspelled Words

Patterns in Spelling

Teaching students how to look for patterns in words is a successful teaching strategy. The following list is derived from spelling words that have been consistently misspelled by students. They have been analyzed then grouped according to patterns. Within those patterns, the words are listed in order from the most difficult to the easiest for needs grouping.

Focusing on spelling patterns and giving small group tests meets student learning needs and provides time for teachers to collect misspelled words from student writing samples. Keep a running record of the words each student misspells. Alternate giving group spelling tests with individual tests, making sure each student is individually tested every other week.

Long a—age, lady, state, face, taste, take, cake, skate, lake, game, grave, plane, same, case, race, escape, made, state, table, able, paper, they, obey, prey, break, main, paid, plain, paint, afraid, straight, always, stays, pray, play, player, way, day, eight, weigh

Short a—apple, sad, black, happy, back, fast, can, class, snack, basket, that, add, than, tax, laugh, passed

Long e—mean, least, leave, beak, each, teacher, dream, meat, meet, peach, sneak, cream, stream, beat, treat, neat, really, peace, sleep, feeling, keep, cheese, week, weak, street, queen, see, seed, agreed, meter, people, money, key, piece, grief

Short e—bed, kept, nest, best, less, spell, help, step, next, left, smell, death, chest, tell, help, sled, credit, better, getting

Long i—while, smile, hide, dried, retire, white, knife, lives, hive, like, bike, five, time, mice, twice, nice, ice, tribe, kite, type, by, why, sky, trying, might, night, light, sign, died, eye

Short i—pinch, sniff, print, with, fifth, brick, which, list, hit, quit, little, wiggle, hid, kid, did, swim, him, miss, sister, give, skin, gym, rich, wish, wind, quick, quit, pick, mix, thin, build, kicked, milk

Long o—poem, over, motel, ocean, open, only, gross, know, show, elbow, told, cold, broke, Coke, note, hope, whole, smoke, joke, oldest, foam, road, coach, roaches, alone, bone, owe, yellow, don't, both

Short o—off, problem, bottom, shot, chop, crop, top, lost, lock, body, soccer, holly, jolly, along, strong

Long u—use, few, unit, bugle, menu

Short u—pull, stuff, upon, number, until, buddy, puppy, thump, pump, under, crunch, pumpkin, hundred

ow—down, drowsy, crowd, flowers, how

or—store, more, horse, story, shorts, world, word, before, favorite

ir—first, third, girl, thirty

ur—nurse, hurt, bury, church, turkey, during, current, fur, burning, sturdy, picture

Patterns in Spelling *(cont.)*

Drop the final e—navigator, eliminating, deceiving, agitating, interfering, dehydrating, devastating, obligation, landscaping, hesitation, dazzling, expiring, grading, hustling, writing, leaving, skating, tasting, waging, sniping, hoping, coming, saving, roping, naming, facing, coping, rating, loping, taping

Change the y to i—currencies, dignified, celebrities, dreariness, inquiries, intensified, knobbier, lavatories, luxurious, liquified, eighties, companies, occupied, qualified, loveliest, likeliest, ceremonies, countries, prettier, colonies, cities, stories, babies, puppies, buddies, worries, dried, fried, tried, cried

Silent consonants—psychiatrist, scholarship, scenario, schedule, solemn, scheme, character, wreckage, orchestrate, righteous, wrath, wrestle, wreath, scent, known, psalm, scene, sought, shepherd, honest, knickers, wrong, write, sign, knife, wrap, know, wrist, gnat, right, school, wreck, knock

ar—artificial, armoire, arbitrate, aquarium, archaic, architect, archive, argument, aristocratic, arduous, arctic, arch, argue, sugar, award, dollar, guard, harvest, farther, article, ark, war, yard, warm, hard, farm, park, mark, army, art

qu—quarrel, tranquil, quotient, quadruple, qualification, quarantine, quadrilateral, relinquish, squadron, Quaker, quota, squealed, square, squash, quarter, question, quickly, quality, equal, quite, quiet, queen, quilt, quick, quack, quickly, equal, quiz, quit

ce/ci—concentrate, introduce, certainly, innocence, precipitate, reception, recession, importance, sociable, apprentice, performance, evidence, incentive, prejudice, sacrifice, entice, ceremony, faucet, dance, recite, justice, juice, rejoice, force, voice, advance, fence, practice, wince, society, violence, advice, office, city, space, ace, ice, lice, once, face, nice, price, rice, race, lace, mice, twice, cent, dice

Add -es—heroes, potatoes, mosquitoes, octopuses, dominoes, cherishes, hoboes, rehashes, sandwiches, addresses, roaches, misses, benches, washes, watches, splashes, dresses, guesses, porches, churches, boxes, taxes, rushes, classes, glasses, foxes, fishes, wishes, goes, riches

Add -s—messages, elephants, revolutions, associations, conquistadors, proclamations, associates, xylophones, examinations, creatures, leaves, flowers, parents, animals, tracks, aunts, autos, soldiers, clothes, months, cans, notes, rides, keys, socks, beds, moths, lives, seeds, jobs, shows

a consonant e—devastate, communicate, exaggerate, hallucinate, concentrate, nauseate, infiltrate, punctuate, associate, segregate, masquerade, escape, skate, chase, grave, village, landscape, voyage, package, investigate, evacuate, persuade, parade, cake, age, game, made, state, take, case, plane, male, flame, grade

er—conservation, different, soldier, shepherd, eradicate, erroneous, defer, offered, concert, poverty, error, person, serve, every, Webster, Germany, energy, camera, winter, nerves, iceberg, were, where, very, germ, fern, water, ever, sister, ruler

i consonant e—porcupine, civilize, quarantine, insecticide, pantomime, acquire, sapphire, perspire, familiarize, ostracize, baptize, chimes, surprise, smile, retire, white, wine, guide, precise, describe, pine, hide, bike, kite, time, ride, dime, hike, five, fire

Patterns in Spelling *(cont.)*

ie/ei—unbelievable, chandelier, cavalier, reindeer, frontier, premier, handkerchief, caffeine, hygiene, debrief, Beirut, grieve, believe, friend, receive, soldier, ceiling, either, cashier, pierced, protein, disbelief, review, weight, chief, pier, tier, brief, grief, thief, belief, relief, pie, die, view

oo—heirloom, preschooler, bassoon, monsoon, typhoon, paratrooper, caboose, kangaroos, zoology, Aroostook, balloon, crooked, maroon, bloom, gloom, school, brook, mushroom, cartoon, cocoon, food, cook, book, good, room, look, moon, roof, wood, boot

ou—mysterious, contagious, suspicious, melodious, strenuous, ridiculous, devoured, boisterous, courageous, igneous, trouble, thousand, nervous, famous, nourish, court, thought, country, young, routine, house, four, your, out, mouth, tour, pour, soup, about, South

oi/oy—turquoise, tabloid, asteroid, paranoid, Polaroid, turmoil, disappoint, corduroy, Rolls Royce, employed, sirloin, tenderloin, choice, voice, spoil, avoid, appoint, noise, destroy, annoy, oil, coin, join, toy, void, boil, soil, toil, point

double the final consonant—periodically, flammable, enthusiastically, critically, continually, occasionally, intentionally, eventfully, initially, dropped, biggest, beginning, batting, hitting, digging, hopping, getting, running, swimming, popping, jogging, mopping, stirred, planning, shopping, bragging, stopped, rotten, wrapped, hidden

o consonant e—wardrobe, artichoke, provoke, parole, palindrome, monotone, antelope, stethoscope, decompose, devote, smoke, whole, alone, explode, chrome, postpone, tombstone, envelope, diagnose, enclose, code, rode, home, rose, joke, Coke, note, hope, bone, owe

ph/gh = f—phosphorous, sapphire, laughter, autograph, paragraph, paraphernalia, philosophy, physician, phenomenon, phosphate, laughed, graph, microphone, sphere, photograph, paragraph, physical, Philadelphia, metamorphic, Philippines, phone, tough, photo, rough, graph, phony, phrase, Philip, laugh

silent gh—foresight, copyright, height, enlighten, neighed, distraught, bought, freight, hindsight, weighed, bought, caught, fought, sought, thought, thigh, straight, almighty, delight, fight, light, might, tight, sight, quite, bright, high, night, sigh

ee/ea = long e—guaranteed, proofread, nominee, jamboree, referee, refugee, exceed, concealed, underneath, colleague, realized, kneel, squeak, disagree, degree, treaty, proceed, mislead, screen, fifteen, Halloween, beard, bee, free, knee, sea, tree, pea, tea, see, bead, beef, hear

tion/sion/cian—petition, beautician, ammunition, coalition, physician, transmission, musician, suspicion, technician, pediatrician, commission, attraction, perception, division, expression, addition, ambition, audition, magician, nutrition, permission, collection, organization, expedition, competition, definition, position, action, tuition, portion, notion, donation, fraction, election, nation, mission, caution

Spelling Errors Tally Sheet

Use this chart to document children's spelling development. Spelling errors can be analyzed and appropriate instruction planned by implementing this sheet. Checkpoints are scheduled throughout the year to specifically analyze each child's spelling progress. Keep the spelling errors tally sheet in the student's file, communicating results with the child and parent at conferences.

Spelling Errors

Name: ______________________

Category	Paper Date	Paper Date	Paper Date	Paper Date	Paper Date
Phonetic					
Left out a pronounced letter					
Left out a silent letter					
Reversed a letter					
Added a letter					
Double consonant					
Substitute a consonant					
Substitute a vowel					
Vowel pattern					
Homonym					
Plural, Possessive, Contraction					
Other					

Name: ______________________________ Date: ____________________

Spelling Words Activity List

Three of the following activities are to be completed and handed in after taking your spelling test. You may complete more than three if you wish. Hand in all activities together, stapled, with everything labeled. Read all of your work to make sure that it reflects your time and effort. Proof, check, and correct all work for proper use of capitals and punctuation before handing it in.

_________ 1. Write your word list in alphabetical order.

_________ 2. Write each word in a complete sentence or write a paragraph using each word. Make sure your paragraph has a beginning, middle, and end.

_________ 3. Complete a word map. The map gives a synonym and antonym, a definition, and a sentence using the word.

_________ 4. Spelling Poster—Using a piece of white construction paper, write your spelling words randomly on the paper in pencil, trying to cover as much area as possible. Double check your spelling of the words put on your paper. Trace the words with brightly colored markers or crayons. Then outline the words with at least three different colors. Try to completely fill your paper.

_________ 5. Make a picture using each spelling word three times. You could draw animals, scenes, or abstracts with your words.

_________ 6. Make a word search using graph paper. Have a friend complete your word search. Grade your friend's attempt.

_________ 7. Make a word scramble. Have a friend complete your word scramble. Grade your friend's attempt.

_________ 8. Write each word three times saying the letters out loud as you write them.

_________ 9. Group or categorize your words by recognizable patterns.

_________ 10. Make a graph showing the number of letters in each of your spelling words.

REMEMBER

Turn all of your work in at one time when you take your test.

Do not turn in work in bits and pieces. Be sure your name is on each page.

Staple all work together by placing one staple in the upper left hand corner.

Give this to each student at the beginning of the year to assess math computation abilities. Keep the assessment on file for reference during the first parent/child conference. A grade is not given for this, but it is used as an initial checkpoint.

Name: ______________________________ Date: ______________

Math Computation Skills Assessment

1. Write the word form of 8,376. ______________________________

   ____

2. Write the expanded form of 5,408. ______________________________

   ____

3. Roman Numerals: I = _____ C = _____ X = _____ V = _____

4. Finish these patterns.

   0, 2, 4, 6, ___, ___, ___ 4, 8, 12, ___, ___, ___

   5, 10, 15, 20, ___, ___, ___ 27, 30, 33, 36, ___, ___, ___

   88, 80, 72, 64, ___, ___, ___ 32, 37, 42, ___, ___, ___

   0, 1/4, 2/4, 3/4, ___, ___, ___ 6.50, 6.75, 7.00, 7.25, ___, ___, ___

5. You have $1.00 and decide to buy a candy bar for $.39. How much change do you have left over? ______________________________

6. You buy three candy bars for 28 cents each. How much do you have to pay for three? ______________________________

7. 346 + 152

8. 508 + 317

9. 267 + 894

10. 563 − 421

11. 92 − 65

12. 55 − 18

13. 27 + 4 + 13 + 6

14. 38 + 5 + 10 + 42

15. 46,177 + 8,610 + 94,345

16. $49.18 + $49.18 + $49.18

17. 706 − 38

18. 430 − 287

19. 624 − 598

20. 41,240 − 13,841

21. $4.50 − $1.46

22. 4 x 7

23. 21 x 3

24. $3 + 2\frac{1}{2}$ = _______

25. $4 - 1\frac{1}{4}$ = _______

26. 148 x 5 = _______

27. 43 x 62

28. 517 x 28

29. 370 x 56

30. $4\overline{)20}$

31. $3\overline{)14}$

32. $5\overline{)75}$

This sheet is given to students every two weeks. All students try to work as many problems as they can in a ten minute period. Initially, grades are not given. It is used as a tool to help students memorize the multiplication facts.

- -

Name: ______________________________ Date: ______________

Multiplication Facts Sheet

1.	0 x 9	3 x 8	5 x 7	7 x 6	9 x 5	1 x 4	2 x 3	4 x 2	6 x 1	8 x 0
2.	0 x 8	3 x 7	5 x 6	7 x 5	9 x 4	1 x 3	2 x 2	4 x 1	6 x 0	8 x 9
3.	0 x 5	3 x 4	5 x 3	7 x 2	9 x 1	1 x 0	2 x 9	4 x 8	6 x 7	8 x 6
4.	0 x 3	3 x 2	5 x 1	7 x 0	9 x 9	1 x 8	2 x 7	4 x 6	6 x 5	8 x 4
5.	0 x 1	3 x 0	5 x 9	7 x 8	9 x 7	1 x 6	2 x 5	4 x 4	6 x 3	8 x 2
6.	0 x 0	3 x 9	5 x 8	7 x 7	9 x 6	1 x 5	2 x 4	4 x 3	6 x 2	8 x 1
7.	0 x 4	3 x 3	5 x 2	7 x 1	9 x 0	1 x 9	2 x 8	4 x 7	6 x 6	8 x 5
8.	0 x 2	3 x 1	5 x 0	7 x 9	9 x 8	1 x 7	2 x 6	4 x 5	6 x 4	8 x 3
9.	0 x 6	3 x 5	5 x 4	7 x 3	9 x 2	1 x 1	2 x 0	4 x 9	6 x 8	8 x 7
10.	0 x 7	3 x 6	5 x 5	7 x 4	9 x 3	1 x 2	2 x 1	4 x 0	6 x 9	8 x 8

This type of assessment should be given at least once a month to determine the level of computational skills at which a student is working. Students are instructed to complete as many of the problems as they understand, knowing that this is not a graded test, but a checkpoint of their progress. This form also provides a review of skills so that students can practice all four of the basic operations.

Name: ______________________________ Date: ______________

Ladder Math I

1. $34 + 25$
2. $12 + 53 + 36$
3. $79 + 54$
4. $734 + 876$
5. $74 - 33$
6. $62 - 46$
7. $60 - 28$
8. $346 - 158$
9. $4{,}602 - 1{,}734$
10. 5×4
11. 7×8
12. 20×4
13. 32×2
14. 641×3
15. 89×7
16. 439×6
17. 53×42
18. 63×10
19. 435×68
20. $4\overline{)12}$
21. $8\overline{)72}$
22. $3\overline{)19}$
23. $7\overline{)61}$
24. $5\overline{)427}$
25. $10\overline{)86}$
26. $12\overline{)3{,}520}$
27. $33\overline{)50{,}729}$

Name: ______________________________ Date: ______________

Ladder Math II

1. 93 + 3
2. 29 + 18
3. 176 + 512
4. 382 + 562
5. 47 + 606
6. 62 + 35 + 17
7. 8,967 + 3,437
8. $3.85 + .59
9. 58 − 43
10. 42 − 7
11. 52 − 5
12. 85 − 28
13. 60 − 44
14. 759 − 463
15. 842 − 375
16. 800 − 512
17. 203 − 25
18. $7.06 − 5.08
19. 978 − 49
20. 7,135 − 2,816
21. 6 x 7
22. 76 x 4
23. 65 x 8
24. 700 x 6
25. $6.90 x 8
26. 27 x 83
27. 79 x 36
28. 90 x 50
29. 408 x 62
30. 745 x 800
31. 7,364 x 38
32. 3) 157
33. 9,478 ÷ 5 = ________
34. 835 − (6 x 8) =

Name: ______________________________ Date: ______________

Mid-Year Math Assessment

Finish these patterns.

1. 6, 8, 10, 12, ____ , ____ , ____
2. 15, 18, 21, 24, ____ , ____ , ____
3. 90, 80, 70, ____ , ____ , ____
4. 60, 55, 50, 45, ____ , ____ , ____
5. 4, 8, 12, 16, ____ , ____ , ____
6. 36, 33, 30, 27, ____ , ____ , ____

Write the word name for each number.

7. 849 = ______________________________
8. 1,210 = ______________________________
9. 36 = ______________________________

Write the expanded form for each number.

10. 725 = ______________________________
11. 3,691 = ______________________________
12. 204 = ______________________________

Round the following numbers to the nearest ten.

13. 32 = ________ 14. 67 = ________ 15. 96 = ________

Solve.

16.	17.	18.	19.	20.
$1.00 – .28	123 + 456	789 + 17	69 – 27	35 – 18

21.	22.	23.	24.	25.
753 – 620	894 – 77	8 x 3	10 x 6	14 x 2

26. 12 ÷ 4 = 27. 9 ÷ 3 = 28. 30 ÷ 5 =

Compare each set of numbers using < , > , or = .

29. 4/6 ________ 1/6
30. 0.3 ________ 0.5
31. 2/10 ________ 8/10
32. 3/3 ________ 1
33. 1/2 ________ 3/4
34. 4/4 ________ 2/2

Name: ______________________________ Date: ______________

Challenging Mid-Year Math Assessment

Solve each problem and record your answers on a separate sheet.

Write the following numbers in word form and expanded form.

1. 690,458
2. 12,703

Write the Roman numerals for each of the following:

3. 67
4. 150
5. 29

6. Write the ordinals from first to eleventh.

Round off these numbers to the nearest hundred.

7. 381
8. 1,702

Write the word name of the following numbers.

9. 0.12
10. 39.05

Solve.

11. 6,009 − 185
12. $482.00 − 105.36
13. 40,128 + 82,907
14. 45.69 + 63.86
15. 32 x 34
16. $16.56 x 8
17. 76 x 84

18. 606 ÷ 6 = ________
19. 53 ÷ 9 = ________
20. $6.95 ÷ 5 = ________

21. 8.4 + 6.35 + 10.08 = ________
22. 5,263 – 1,874 = ________

23. 63 days = _______ weeks
24. 2 hours 10 minutes = ________ minutes

25. 96 hours = ____ days
26. (2÷8) + (4÷8) = ____
27. (5+6) – (2+6) ____

Compare using >, <, or =.

28. 50.05 ____ 5.05
29. 28,409 ____ 29,408
30. 4.1 ____ 3.98

31. 5 cm ____ 500 mm
32. 4 ÷ 5 ____ 2 ÷ 5
33. 15 ÷ 10 ___ 15 ÷ 100

34. 8 ÷ 4 ____ 3
35. 0.4 ____ 4 ÷ 100
36. 6 ÷ 12 ____ 2 ÷ 4

37. 15 inches ____ 1 foot
38. 2 yards ____ 6 feet

Observing and Analyzing Art

One important area of a child's educational curriculum is art. Children can be taught to analyze works of art and use appropriate terms to describe them. The following descriptive words should be written on a chart placed beside the works of art being critiqued.

Lines: choppy, curved, diagonal, fuzzy, heavy, horizontal, jagged, sharp, straight, thick, thin, vertical

Shapes: circles, squares, triangles, rectangles

Textures: rough, shiny, smooth, soft

Balance: symmetrical, asymmetrical

Colors:

Neutral—brown, black, white,
Warm—red, orange, yellow
Cool—blue, green, violet
Opposites—blue and orange
red and green
yellow and violet

Space: deep space, shallow space, flat space

NAME ____________________ DATE __________

NAME OF ARTIST ____________________ MEDIUM __________

TITLE OF WORK ____________________ SIZE __________

1. First Glance—Is the work realistic (looks real), stylized (recognizable, not real), or abstract? ____________________

   ____

2. DESCRIPTION—"What Do You See?"

   List the main objects that you see. Be objective. Write down every fact that you observe.

   Is the work balanced? ____________________

   What is the focal point? ____________________

   ____

3. ANALYSIS—"How is the Work Organized?"

   List the main types of each:

   lines ____________________

   shapes ____________________

   textures ____________________

   colors ____________________

   light and dark areas ____________________

   use of space ____________________

Science Through Exploration

Traditional science instruction focuses on the teacher informing students about a particular science concept. Teachers attempt to pass on to their pupils their mastery over the content as they see it. Then, students verify and apply the knowledge in the form of answering questions and solving problems from a textbook in preparation for a test. Students are often discouraged from taking any detour from the teacher's ideas.

The traditional method offers little student involvement or exploration, and students are usually unfamiliar with how scientific knowledge is generated. Consequently, traditional teaching practices appear to fail in helping students gain conceptual understandings consistent with the views of scientists.

The following practices may help students develop important science concepts.

First, teachers must develop an understanding of the scientist's views, the children's views, and their own personal views in relation to the concept. Ascertaining the student's existing views and alternative conceptions can be very valuable.

Next, a teacher needs to use language familiar to the learner in clearly explaining the procedures of the lesson. During the lesson, provide activities that focus the child's attention on the concept and allow free exploration. Monitor students during the exploration time. Observe their actions and reactions, encourage them to think about what is happening and how it is occurring, and assist students in interpreting their responses.

Finally, allow students to explore the concept in a relevant context. Think of ways to relate the concept to everyday life, to the child's existing ideas, and to the child's relationships with others. In fact, allow and encourage students to interact with others. Permit students to debate the pros and cons of their current views with each other. Act as a guide by helping students link their current experience with their existing ideas. Encourage students to raise questions and engage in further problem solving. As students investigate practice problems, test a hypothesis, reflect on and solve problems, they will be able to gain a more scientific opinion of the concept.

There are times when it may be necessary to inform a student and then verify that knowledge with a demonstration. For example, the traditional method may be appropriate when a teacher must identify and define new terms or when safety procedures must be discussed. Nevertheless, a child's learning experience must respond to the fact that children have existing ideas. Students often learn better by manipulating materials, exploring their environment, and by interacting with others.

Science Resources That Support Exploration

These resources can provide valuable science materials and workshops for little or no cost. Addresses and publisher information is provided to assist teachers in contacting sources for current booklets and services.

Teacher Created Materials Units

Science Investigations—John and Patty Carratello
All About Science Fairs—John and Patty Carratello
The Human Body—David Jefferies
Rocks and Soil—Janet Hale
Oceans—Mary Ellen Sterling
Ecology—Mary Ellen Sterling

How to Turn Kids On To Science

by B.K. Hixson
Wild Goose Company and GBASE Workshops
Murray, Utah, 1993
Wild Goose Workshops provide samples of chemicals and other necessary materials to conduct science experiments. Instructors knowledgeably guide you through experiments and answer your questions.

Pellets From the Source

3004 Pinewood
Bellingham, WA 98225
This location offers owl pellets and other hands-on science materials at little cost.

Hands-On Nature: Exploring the Environment

by Jenepher Lingelback
Vermont Institute of Natural Resource, 1986
Woodstock, Vermont 05091
This teacher resource book provides a variety of learning activities to help students explore nature.

Science Through Children's Literature: An Integrated Approach

by Carol M. Butzow and John W. Butzow
Teacher Ideas Press, 1989
A teacher resource book that offers science activities related specifically to selected children's literature.

Ranger Rick's Nature Scope Magazines for students

National Wildlife Federation, 1989

Life Science Activities, Earth Science Activities, and Physical Science Activities for Grades 2–8

by Marvin N. Tolman and James O. Morton, 1986
Parker Publishing Company
West Nyack, NY

Boston Museum of Science Rental Kits provide lessons and all materials needed to conduct experiments and investigations.

1-800-722-5487
Museum of Science
Science Park
Boston, MA 02114-1099
Grades 3–6—Electricity and Magnetism, Microscopes, Plants and Seeds, Simple Machines, Solar System, and Weather
Grades 4–8—Ancient Egypt, Just Add Water, Wolves and Humans, Prehistory: Clues to the Past, Rocks and Minerals

This lab provides a model for designing future science lab procedures for children as well as encouraging student exploration and investigation.

Name: ______________________________ Date: ______________

Sample Science Lab: Force and Friction

Materials:

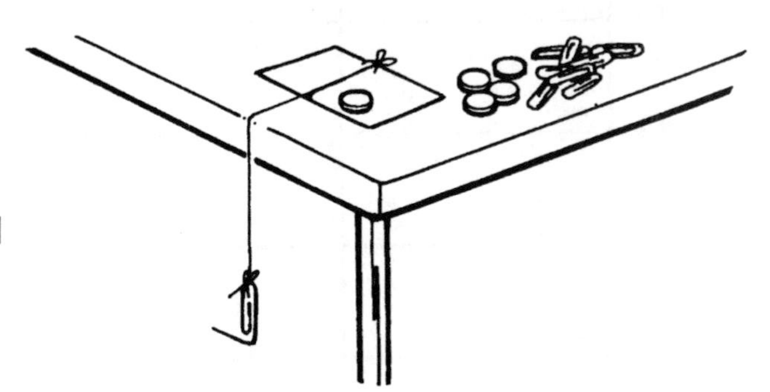

- a piece of thread 12 inches (30 cm) long
- 15 paper clips
- 5 pennies
- 1 – 3" x 5" (8 cm x 13 cm) cardboard card
- graph paper
- a piece of sandpaper

Hypothesis:

How many paper clips will it take to move the index card with no pennies on it?

How many paper clips will it take to move the index card if there are pennies on the card?

Directions:

1. Tie a foot (30 cm) of thread to a 3" x 5" (8 cm x 13 cm) index card.
2. Then bend a paper clip into a hook and tie it to the other end of the thread.
3. Place the card on your desk with the hook hanging about six inches over the edge.
4. If the card does not move, hold the card with a finger and add a paper clip to the hook. Remove your finger and see whether the card moves.
5. If not, add another paper clip. Remove your finger and see whether the card moves now. When the card does move, record your first observation on the graph.
   Predict how many paper clips it will take to move the card and one penny.
6. Put a penny on the index card, and try the experiment again. Add paper clips until the card moves. When the card moves, record the line of force on your graph.
7. Continue adding pennies and paper clips until you reach a five-penny load.

Analysis:

What happened as you added pennies to the card?

Why did that happen?

What can this relate to in real life? If you did this experiment on the moon would the results be the same?

Did you do anything different than the instructions?

Do you have an experiment that you would like to try with the materials?

Connections: Design your own experiment. You may try folding the card or stacking the load of pennies in a single pile. Create a way to record your new data.

Name: ______________________________ Date: ______________

Paper Clip Power

Force vs. Friction Graph

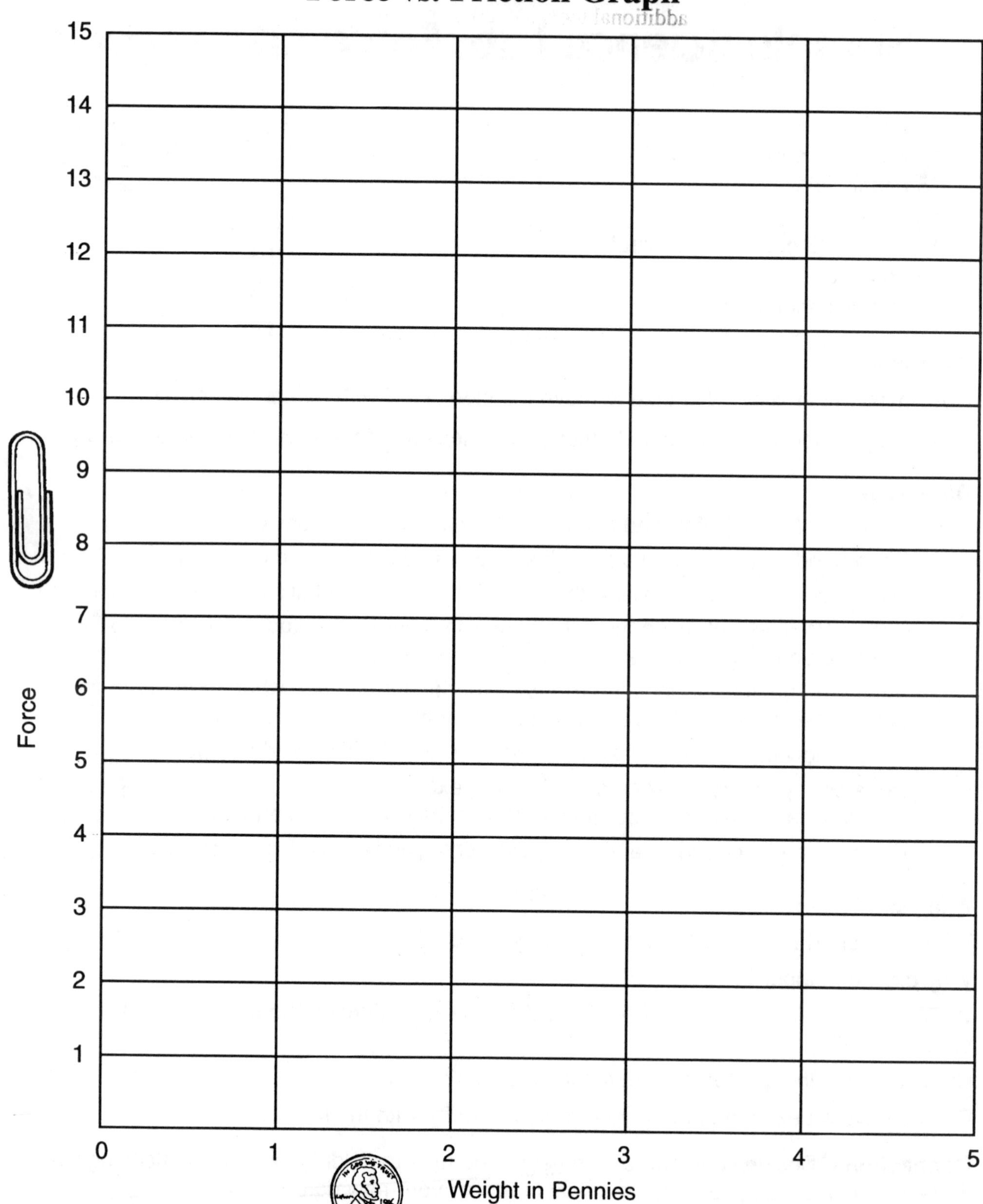

Technology Focus

Taking advantage of the additional tools and opportunities for learning

Each child using the computers, laserdiscs, camera, VCR, and editing equipment

Children understanding and explaining how to use the equipment

Helping others become trained and feel confident in using technology

Now able to access the world through E-mail, Internet, and World Wide Web

Ownership and responsibility of learning given to the student

Leadership from students in communicating what they are learning

On-going training and progress in technological understanding

Generating ideas for meaningful independent studies, multimedia products, and personal goals

Youth critiquing themselves and others, then revising individual and group performances

Finding appropriate ways to integrate technology into units

Original works being submitted for publication

Conducting interviews, videotaping school news, and creating original products

Understanding that computer literacy is important to the child's success in life

Stimulating and challenging students and working cooperatively

Recommended Software Programs:

- *ClarisWorks*
- *HyperStudio*
- *Kid Pix*
- *The Factory*
- *Type to Learn*
- *The Cruncher*
- *The Incredible Machine*
- *Decisions, Decisions*
- *Multimedia Workshop*
- *My Own Stories*
- *Touchdown Math*
- *The Great Ocean Rescue*
- *Adventures of Jasper Woodbury*
- *Grolier Multimedia Encyclopedia*
- *Math Shop Spotlight*
- *How the West Was Negative One*
- *Storybook Weaver*

Use this form as a checklist to make sure each child is learning to use the technology equipment you have available.

Technology Checklist

Date accomplished:

Name:																	
Operated the Laserdisc																	
Used the Barcode Reader																	
Page of Fonts Saved on Disk																	
Edited a Paragraph																	
Short Story Saved on Disk																	
Word Processing Card																	
Claris—Drew a Design																	
Claris—Used the Painting																	
Used Clip Art																	
Designed Personal Checks																	
Storybook Weaver/My Own Stories																	
Completed a Grolier Task Card																	
Completed a CRUNCHER Graph																	
Claris—Spreadsheet Card																	
Scanned a Visual																	
Used Scanner Options																	
Taped with the Camera																	
Used the Camera as a VCR																	
Used a VCR to View Tape																	
Edited Videotape																	
Copied From Disk to Video																	
Made a Hardbacked Book																	
Type to Learn																	
Touchdown Math																	
The Factory																	
The Incredible Machine																	
Math Shop: Weights and Measures																	
Claris – Database Card																	

Technology Task Cards

The widespread use of computers in school and at home dictates that training in technology be included in a progressive educational program. The following Technology Task Cards lead students through the basic elements of Claris Works word processing, spreadsheets, and databases. Children enjoy these activities and usually master them quickly. The Task Cards have proven to be effective tools by helping each child acquire basic computer competency.

Word Processing Task Card

1. Open Hard Drive. Open Claris Works—Word Processing.
2. Type the following paragraph. Remember to push tab to indent.

We the people of the United States, in order to form a more perfect Union, establish justice, insure domestic tranquility, provide for the common defense, promote the general welfare, and secure the blessings of liberty to ourselves and our posterity, do ordain and establish this Constitution of the United States of America.

3. When you have finished typing, highlight the paragraph.
   Change the font to Zapf Chancery.
   Change the size to 18.
4. Go to Edit—Spelling—Check Document. Correct any misspelled words.
5. Change the size of the words "We the people" to 36.
6. Copy the entire paragraph and paste it below the first one.
7. Center the second paragraph.
8. Go to Format—Insert Header. Type your first and last name in Bold on the right side of the header.
9. Go to Format—Insert Footer. Click the center button on the ruler bar.
   Go to Edit—Insert Page #.
10. Go to File—Save. Click on Desktop. Double click on your disk. Name this assignment "Word Processing." Click on Save.
11. Print this assignment. Go to File—Print.

Technology Task Cards *(cont.)*

Spreadsheet Task Card

1. Open Hard Drive. Open Claris Works—Spreadsheet.
2. Go to Format—Document. Set the margins at .75, the columns size at 50 and the rows size at 20.
3. Select the Helvetica font and size 9.
4. Type in the following inventory list.

   Chairs 124, Tables 16, File cabinets 5, Desks 102, Bulletin boards 20, Chalkboards 7, Dictionaries 50, Animal cages 5, and Small cubbies 182.
5. Highlight all of the information. Go to Options—Make Chart. Choose Bar Graph and Horizontal. Click on OK.
6. Now, situate the graph from column C through column H and from row 1 to row 19.
7. Go to File—Page Setup. Choose the icon of a man.
8. Go to File—Save. Click on Desktop. Double click on your disk. Name this assignment "Spreadsheet." Click on Save.
9. Print this assignment. Go to File—Print.

Technology Task Cards *(cont.)*

Database Task Card

1. Open HD—Claris Works—Database—OK
2. At the Define Fields screen, make sure the Text button is selected. Then, type
   Last Name—Enter
   First Name—Enter
   Address—Enter
   City—Enter
   State—Enter
3. Select the Number button. Type Zip—Enter—Done.
4. Now it is time to enter your data. Do not push return to move to the next field! Push tab. To move to the next record, go to Edit—New Record.
5. List the names and addresses of 3 people you know.
6. After you have finished entering the records for 3 people, save them as "Addresses."
7. Go to File—New—Word Processing—OK.
8. To add in First Name, go to File—Open—Addresses—Open.
9. Click on your letter. Go to File—Mail Merge. When it shows a box with Addresses, click on OK. Click on First Name and then Insert Field.
10. Each time you want to insert one of the field names, click on the one that you want to use and click on Insert Field.
11. You will be typing the following letter.
    First Name Last Name
    Address
    City, State Zip
    Dear__________
    There is good news in ____________ today! I am typing you a letter at school. I am going to use ClarisWorks Databases to insert your name and address into different places on this letter. What do you think about that?
    Yours truly,
12. When you are finished with the letter, click on Print Merge. The computer will make three copies of the letter, each one personalized for each person.

Technology Task Cards *(cont.)*

Grolier Scavenger Hunt task cards are used to conduct research related to your literature-based thematic units. Before providing the task cards, teach students to use the *Grolier Multimedia Encyclopedia.* Students enjoy working on these individually or with a partner.

Number the Stars—Grolier Hunt

Title List

1. Find Denmark. Denmark is located between which two bodies of water?
2. What is the capital of Denmark?

Word Search

3. Open Holocaust. How many Jews were massacred by the Nazi regime during World War II?

Timeline

4. Find 1939. What country did Germany invade, beginning World War II?
5. Who was the U.S. President in 1939?

Maps

6. Open Denmark. Find Copenhagen. If I were in Goteborg, Sweden, what direction would I travel to get to Copenhagen?
7. Name the country that borders Denmark to the south.

Sounds

8. Open Famous Speeches. Listen to Neil Armstrong's Apollo II mission speech. Finish writing his famous quote. "That's one small step for man, ______________ ______________________________________."

Knowledge Explorer—Grolier Hunt

9. Open Science—Space Exploration. Play this. It is longer than you might expect. The first space satellite, Sputnik I, was launched by what country?

Pictures

10. Open History—World War II—Persecution of the Warsaw Jews. Then look at the Germans' march into Czechoslovakia. Put a ✔ when you have explored this. Open Politics—Political Figures—European Political Leaders—Adolf Hitler. Read.

Videos

11. Open Historical Events and Personalities—Adolf Hitler. Play this video. Open World War II, Fall of France. Play this video. Put a ✔ when you have explored this.

Animations

12. Open Mechanical Processes—aircraft controls. Name the three lines of flight for an aircraft.

    (a) ______________ (b) ______________ (c) ______________

Technology Task Cards *(cont.)*

Revolution – Grolier Hunt

Write your answers on an index card.

Title List

1. Find and open Green Mountain Boys. Commanded by Ethan Allen, the Green Mountain Boys captured Fort ____________ from the British.

Multimedia Maps

Click on Early American History: The American Revolution

2. On July 3rd, George Washington was named ____________ of the Continental Army.
3. After the Declaration of Independence was passed, the British strategy was to split the colonies in half and isolate ____________.
4. The ____________ ended the Revolutionary War on September 3, 1783.

Pictures

Click on History—American Revolution.

5. Soldiers at Valley Forge. Click on the word Caption.

   ____________'s Continental Army spent the winter of 1777–1778 at Valley Forge.

   Click on George Washington's first cabinet. Click on the word Caption. Name two people who served with President Washington.

6. Secretary of State ____________
7. Secretary of the Treasury ____________

Timeline

8. Click on Find Year. Type in 1775—Find. British troops and colonial ____________ clash at ____________ starting the American Revolution.

Maps

Click on States of the U.S.A.—Massachusetts.

9. Name the five states that border Massachusetts.

Sounds

Click on Famous Speeches—Washington, George—Farewell Address.

10. At the beginning of his address, Washington says "Observe good faith and justice toward all nations. Cultivate ____________ and ____________ with all."

Centers

Planning Centers

Learning Centers are typically literature-based instructional activities, although not all learning centers have to be related to the current area of study. Some centers may be broad enough to extend throughout several units so students can have additional opportunities to complete them. Learning centers must address varied ability levels, encourage student interaction, and communicate directions clearly to students. Learning centers provide students with the opportunity to actively explore, make choices, and think about their learning.

Tips for Centers

1. Decide which centers you plan to provide for students and where they will be located.
2. Decide whether each center will be a requirement for all students to complete or whether it is one they may choose as an elective.
3. Make sure each center area is clearly labeled, that the directions are clear, and that the appropriate materials are provided.
4. Post the expected completion time at each center to help keep students on task. Each child is accountable for time spent at a center and is expected to be a diligent worker. Students may ask for an extension in order to complete a center.
5. Decide with your team when center time will be offered. It may help to schedule centers at the same time.
6. If centers are being shared among several classes, determine the number of students allowed to participate at each center at one time.
7. As a group or individually, allow students to preview each center.
8. Determine a consistent plan for rotating students through the centers.
9. Determine what will be an acceptable finished product for each ability level.
10. Brainstorm ways to encourage quality products and independence during center time.
11. As a team, set clear routines, rules, and expectations for center time.
12. Occasionally give brief advertisements for centers that need to be publicized. Students or teachers may model the expections for each center.
13. Determine situations when students will be allowed to choose a center. It can be used as a reward.
14. Model clean up of materials at centers and where to put complete and incomplete work. Teach students to keep the center areas clean!
15. Try to attract parent volunteers who will assist students during center time.
16. Design a Center Checklist to help you keep track of the centers each student has completed, dates when the student began working at the center, the center he or she is currently working on, and possible centers you may steer students toward in the future.
17. Have each child communicate his or her center progress with his or her parents. Make sure the children continue to be challenged to reach their potential.

Center Sharing Contract Form

It is important for students to understand the value of what they are learning and to be able to effectively communicate that knowledge orally or in writing. The following checklist is a valuable tool to help children assess their own performance as they prepare to give a presentation to a group. It provides a guideline for students to follow to ensure that they give extra thought and attention to the effectiveness of their presentation, that they have the necessary materials, have critiqued themselves, and have asked for advice from others.

Student Center Sharing Contract

Before presenting your center work to the other students and teachers, you must first go through and check off items on the following list.

______ 1. I made certain that I followed all of the directions for my center.

______ 2. I have everything that I will need to make my presentation.

______ 3. I have practiced what I am going to present more than three times, and I am very comfortable with what I have to say.

______ 4. I can make my voice loud enough and speak slowly enough so that my audience will be able to hear and understand me.

______ 5. I have gone back over everything on this list before letting my teacher know that I am ready to present my center.

______ 6. After I checked with my teacher, I made a videotape of my presentation.

______ 7. I viewed the video and made improvements. The improvements that I have made include: ______________________________
____

______ 8. I have shared my presentation with at least two other people and have asked them for advice on making it better.

Advisor's Signature __________ Advisor's Signature __________

______ 9. I showed my materials to a teacher. ____________________
Teacher's signature

Center Title ______________________________ Date __________

Student Signature ______________________________

Flannelboard Storytelling Center

This section offers a variety of Center Activity Cards which can be reproduced or laminated for repeated use. Other ideas for centers are available from *Teacher Created Materials: Learning Centers Through the Year* (TCM059), *Weather Learning Center* (TCM1000), *Sea Life Learning Center* (TCM1042), and *Creepy Crawlies Learning Center* (TCM1043)

Students can enjoy using the flannelboard center to re-enact their favorite book or create original flannelboard stories. *The Flannel Board Storytelling Book* by Judy Sierra (The H.W. Wilson Co., 1987) is an excellent resource for stories and character patterns.

Material List:

Permanent markers
Pencils
Scrap paper
Scissors
Various colored felt squares-
8" x 10" (20 cm x 26 cm)
Glue
Flannelboards
Stories for students to use

Flannelboard Story Activity Card

1. Choose a favorite story, use the current literature, or write your own story.
2. Trace the characters from the book on notebook paper or design your own characters.
3. Cut the characters out of the felt, adding details with a permanent marker.
4. Practice telling the story and moving the characters on the flannel board.
5. Fill out the Center Sharing Contract to share your story.

Matrix Puzzles Center

These puzzles are designed to give students opportunities to solve problems. As they become comfortable with this type of puzzle, encourage students to write their own matrix puzzles to share with the class. The matrix solutions can be illustrated using a sentence strip chart.

Matrix Puzzle Activity Card #1

Crumley, Adams, and Wood are an engineer, nurse, and comic book writer. Crumley is not the engineer or nurse. Wood is not the nurse. What job does each person have?

	Crumley	Adams	Wood
Engineer			
Nurse			
Comic Writer			

Matrix Puzzle Activity Card #2

Chris, Alan, Emily, and Jacquelyn are an artist, a salesperson, a chief executive, and a computer programmer. Neither Emily nor Alan is the computer programmer. Jacquelyn is a chief executive. Alan paints and sculpts. What is each person's job?

	Chris	Alan	Emily	Jacquelyn
artist				
sales person				
chief executive				
computer programmer				

Matrix Puzzles Center *(cont.)*

Matrix Puzzle Activity Card #3

Ashley, Carlin, David, and Shanna were eating snacks of ice cream, carrots, bacon, and popcorn. Shanna ate her snack raw. David waited 20 minutes to eat his snack, and it melted. Carlin did not eat the bacon. What snack did each person eat?

	Ashley	Carlin	David	Shanna
ice cream				
carrots				
bacon				
popcorn				

Matrix Puzzle Activity Card #4

April, Krystal, Paul, Scott, and Tyler won prizes at the fair. They won a glove, hat, stuffed animal, helium balloon, and playdough. Paul and Tyler wore their prizes home. April lost hold of her prize, and it sailed high into the air. Scott's playdough was in Paul's glove. What prize did each person win?

	April	Paul	Krystal	Scott	Tyler
glove					
hat					
stuffed animal					
helium balloon					
playdough					

Newspaper Center

Newspaper Center Bulletin Board

Design a bulletin board that includes the following information about parts of a newspaper. This page may also be used as a newspaper guide sheet.

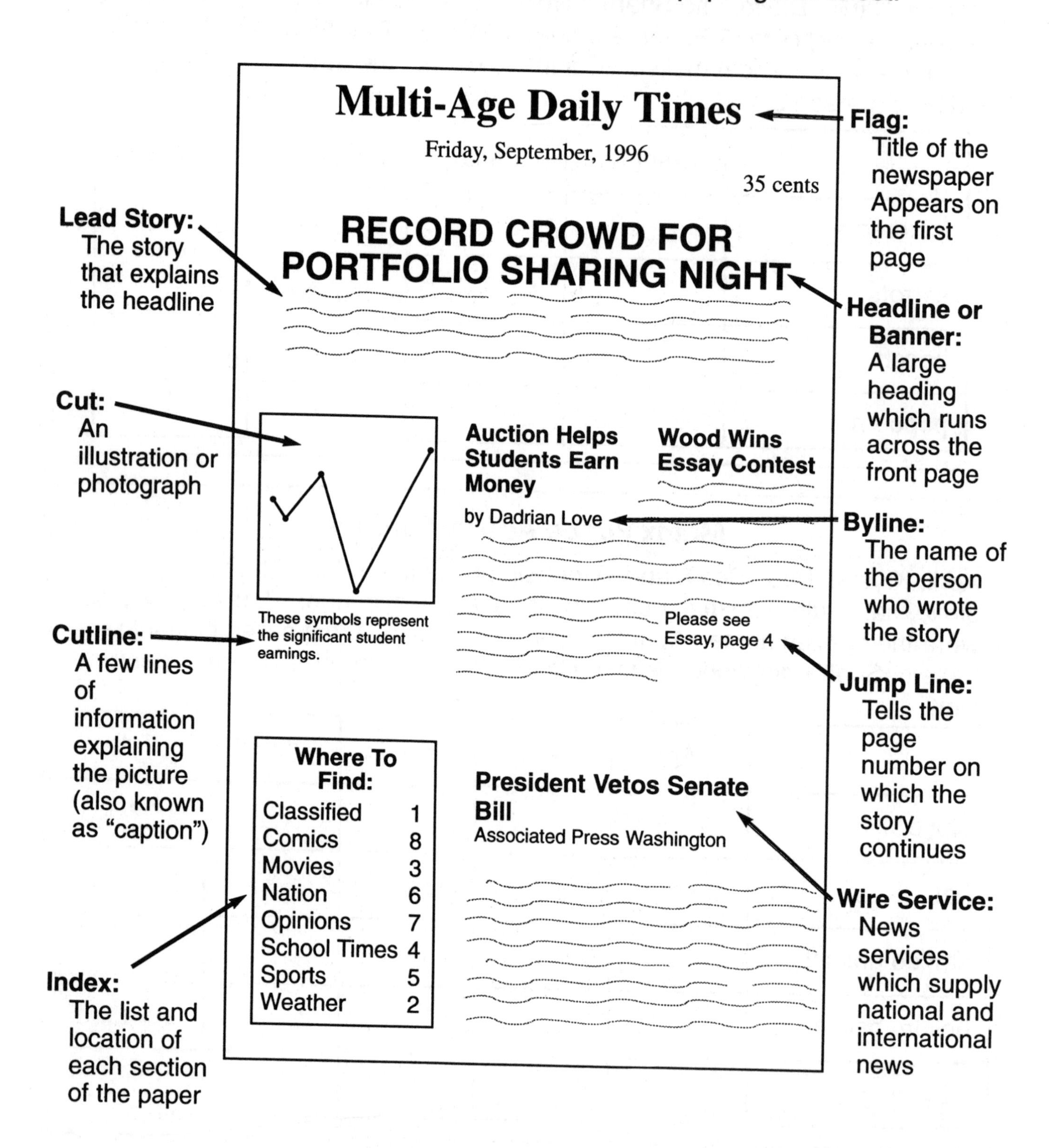

Newspaper Center *(cont.)*

Newspaper Center Activity Card

Directions:

1. Create your own newspaper. Design the front page so that it includes a flag, headline, byline, cut, and cutline.
2. The lead story should answer the questions: Who? What? Why? Where? When? How?
3. After you have designed your rough draft, assess yourself using the Newspaper Assessment Form.
4. Next, ask another classmate to assess your newspaper using the assessment form.
5. Finally, create your final draft on drawing paper or by using the computer.
6. Give the completed final draft to your teacher along with the Newspaper Assessment Form.

Name: ______________________ Newspaper Title: ____________________

Check each item included in your newspaper.

		Self	Peer	Teacher
The lead story explains	Who?			
	What?			
	Why?			
	When?			
	Where			
The newspaper has a	How?			
	Flag?			
	Headline?			
	Byline?			
	Cut?			
	Cutline?			

Parts of a Book Center

Check Bibliography Section for Parts of a Book Center—book sources.

Parts of a Book

You will be using several classroom textbooks to locate information about the title page, table of contents, glossary, and index pages. Please write your answers in the spaces provided. When you have completed this activity, turn your booklet in to your teacher.

Name: ______________________ Date: __________

Name of Activity Card: ______________________

What I learned from this activity: ______________________

____

____

____

Activity Card #1: The Title Page

The title page provides the reader with information about the book's creation. On the title page you learn more than just the book's title!

Study the title page from ________ . Then answer the questions that follow.

1. Where in the book do you find the title page? ______________
2. Who are the authors of the book? ______________
3. Who is the publisher? ______________
4. In what city and state is the publishing company located? __________
5. Name another city outside the U.S. where this book is published.

   ____
6. What does an illustrator do? ______________

Parts of a Book Center *(cont.)*

Activity Card #2: The Title Page Challenge

Now you are ready for a challenge. For this activity use a book of your own choice. Then answer the questions that follow. Remember to use appropriate capital letters.

1. What is the title of the book you chose? ______________________
2. Who is the author of the book? ______________________
3. What is the name of the book's illustrator? ______________________
4. Name the publishing company of this book. ______________________
5. Where is the publishing company located? ______________________

Bonus Question

6. Name the title of another book with the same publishing company.

   ____

Activity Card #3: Table of Contents

The table of contents is found at the front of a book. It lists the chapters in a book and the page numbers on which each chapter begins. Study the table of contents in your reading textbook. Then answer the questions below.

1. There are __________ units in this book.
2. What unit begins on page _________ ?
3. On what page would you find a poem? __________

   Name of poem? ______________________
4. Are there any award-winning books noted in the Table of Contents?

   ____
5. What are the names of two award-winning books? ______________________

   ____
6. On what page does the glossary begin? ______________________

Parts of a Book Center *(cont.)*

Activity Card #4: Glossary Challenge

As you have learned, a glossary is like a little dictionary containing words found in your text. Use the glossary in your Reading textbook to answer the following questions.

1. On what page does the glossary begin? ____________________
2. What does "anonymous" mean? ____________________
3. Name the two guide words on page 7. ____________________

   ____
4. If it were in this glossary, the word fish would come right before __________.
5. What four parts of speech are listed in the glossary? ____________________
6. Name one word from the glossary that can be used as either a noun or verb.

   ____
7. What is the first entry word found in this glossary? ____________________
8. What is the last entry word found in this glossary? ____________________
9. Name the letters of the alphabet that are not listed in this glossary. __________

   ____

Activity Card #5: The Index Challenge

An index lists the main topics covered in a book. It is found at the back of a book. It lists entries in alphabetical order. Page numbers are also listed to help you find the topics. Find the index in your Mathematics textbook. Then answer the questions.

1. Facts about cones are found on pages ____________________.
2. You could learn about flowcharts by reading pages____________________.
3. If the word toenails were added to this index, it would be found just before the word ____________________.
4. Information about dividing by tens can be found on pages ______________.
5. The first entry in the index is ____________________.
6. How many different pages let you explore? ____________________
7. Addition with money can be found on pages ____________________.
8. Information about pictographs can be found on pages ______________.
9. The last entry word in this index is____________________.

Body Systems Center

Use reference books to find the answers to the following questions. On a separate piece of paper answer each question with a complete sentence.

1. Approximately how many bones are in a human skeleton?
2. What organ is mainly responsible for helping someone breathe?
3. Which system is responsible for moving blood throughout your body?
4. Name three foods that contain carbohydrates.
5. When you swallow, what flaps of muscle keep food from entering your lungs?
6. What are the names of three substances that make up your blood?
7. What are the bones that run down your back called?
8. When you start to bleed, what element causes the bleeding to clot, or stop?
9. Where do waste food products that can't be digested in the small intestine go?
10. What is the name of the muscle that helps humans breathe?
11. What type of cells provide protection from diseases?
12. What is the name of the tube that connects your mouth to your stomach?
13. What is the name of the body system that keeps you breathing?
14. What is the name of the blood vessels that carry fresh blood away from the heart?
15. What is the name of the set of bones that protects the brain?
16. What are the names of the air sacs at the end of the bronchial tubes?
17. Which system is responsible for helping you break food down into smaller parts?
18. What is the name of a fixed joint, where the bones just stay in place?
19. What is the name of the gas that humans exhale, or breathe out?
20. What are the bones in your fingers and toes called?
21. Name one hinge joint and tell what it allows to happen.
22. What is the name of the blood vessels that bring "dirty" blood to the heart?
23. What is the name of the gas that humans breathe in?
24. What are the names of the three bones that make up your arm?
25. What is another name for the voice box in your body?
26. What is the name of the organ that removes waste products from your blood?
27. What is the name of a mineral that helps to make your bones hard?
28. What are the strong, flexible straps that hold your bones together called?
29. Besides fixed joints, name four other types of joints.

Body Systems Center *(cont.)*

Materials List: resources containing information about body systems, materials for modeling: clay, papier mâché, paper

Body Systems Activity Card

1. On a separate piece of paper answer each of the questions with a complete sentence.
2. Then choose a body system.
3. Next find out how the system works. Use reference books and videos
4. Learn at least five new words.
5. Create a three-dimensional model illustrating one of the body systems.
6. Share your model with the class.
7. Give a detailed description of how the system works. Use the five new words during your presentation to the class.

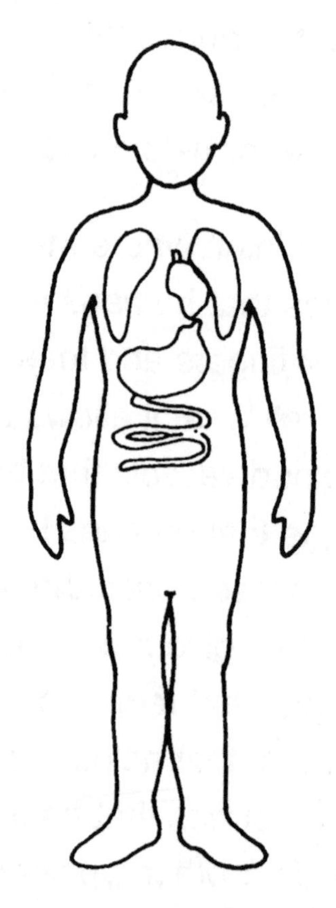

Poetry Center

Provide different examples of poetry types on a bulletin board display. Also provide books of poetry and a variety of writing paper, construction paper, colored pencils, crayons, and pens for writing and illustrating fun.

Student created poems can be hung on a "Poet-Tree" created from an artificial Christmas tree or a bulletin board tree.

Choose one type of poem to create from the following suggestions, then write and illustrate your poem before displaying. Remember to capitalize the first word of each line of poetry!

". . . is" Poems
Happiness is making a good grade because you gave it your best.
Happiness is a tasty meal and a warm bed to sleep in.

Hink-Pinks (2 one-syllable rhyming words)
Mouse House

Color Poems
(*Hailstones and Halibut Bones.* Mary O'Neill. Doubleday and Company, Inc., 1961)
Red is a stop sign on my neighborhood street.
Red is my skin burned by the heat.

Free Form Poem
Sleepiness

Heavy eyes
Nodding
No idea
What's
Going
On.

Preposition Poem
Fly

In the door
On the food
Over the table
Across the room
Upon the wall
Under my fly swatter

Diamante
Line 1: 1 word: noun/subject
Line 2: 2 words: adjectives describing the subject
Line 3: 3 "-ing" words about the subject
Line 4: 4 nouns (2 for the subject, 2 for the opposite)
Line 5: 3 "-ing" words about the opposite noun
Line 6: 2 adjectives describing the opposite
Line 7: 1 noun/opposite of subject
Your poem should end up in the shape of a diamond.

Haiku
(3 lines, 5-7-5 syllables, about nature)

Clouds rolling up high
Trees swaying in the strong breeze
It's starting to rain.

Limerick (5 lines, a-a-b-b-a rhyme)
Roshan, David, Carlos, and Richard
Wrote a story that was quite observed.
They read it aloud.
The audience was proud.
Is it possible they believed what they heard?

Tanka
(5 lines, 5-7-5-7-7 syllables)

Caleb wrote stories.
To enhance his creations.
Drew illustrations.
With brushes, paints, and his pen.
He wrote stories now and then.

Cinquain
(5 lines, 2-4-6-8-2 syllables)

Design
Symmetrical
Standing, Sparkling, Glowing
Made of crackers, icing, candy
Sweet House

Homework

Sample Homework Choices

Reproduce and laminate copies of these task cards to send home in student homework folders. Give each child one card for homework. Make sure the skills have been taught during class. Most students can complete each task card.

Revolution Homework Card 1, Plurals

Plural means more than one. Make the following words plural. Write each plural word on your paper.

1. executive
2. patriot
3. delegate
4. oath
5. amendment
6. sentry
7. territory
8. colony
9. speech
10. child
11. assembly
12. city
13. minuteman
14. branch

Revolution Homework Card 2, Possessive

Possessive shows when someone has ownership. Use apostrophes to show ownership with each phrase.

Example: Mrs. Bolton's truck

1. Virginias and Georgias delegates
2. Paul Reveres jobs
3. John Hancocks signature
4. Sam Adams loyal dog
5. John Hancocks fancy clothes
6. Patrick Henrys speech
7. Southern Colonies plantations
8. Washingtons army

Sample Homework Choices *(cont.)*

Revolution Homework Card 3, Past tense

A past tense verb is used to show that the action has already occurred. Write the following verbs to show past tense.

Example: go—went

1. warn
2. ride
3. write
4. vote
5. notice
6. give
7. approve
8. revise
9. convince
10. ring
11. marry
12. throw

Revolution Homework Card 4, Syllables

Divide the following words into syllables, marking the stressed syllable. You may use a dictionary. Example: Con-sti-tú-tion

1. musket
2. declaration
3. independence
4. Concord
5. Lexington
6. Philadelphia
7. patriot
8. Indian
9. Loyalist
10. camoflage
11. knapsack
12. persistent
13. traitor
14. bayonet
15. triumphant

Sample Homework Choices *(cont.)*

Revolution Homework Card 5, Capitals and commas

Write the following sentences with correct capitals and commas.

1. the boston tea party happened on december 16 1773.
2. the first continental congress met on October 26 1774.
3. the united states and great britain signed the treaty of paris on september 3 1783.
4. the declaration of independence was adopted on july 4 1776.

Revolution Homework Card 6, Compound sentences

Compound sentences combine two related sentences into one sentence. They often use the words and, but, for, or, nor, so, and yet. Combine the two sentences each time to form a compound sentences.

Example: Brandon plays baseball, and his mother cheers.

1. Sam refused to ride a horse. John convinced him to try.
2. Men dressed like Indians. They threw tea off the ship.
3. Ben invented many things. We remember Ben today.
4. Men disagreed with the taxes. They refused to pay them.
5. King George acted like he wasn't worried about the war. He didn't know how to make the people in America behave.

Sample Homework Choices *(cont.)*

Art Graph

You will need 2 sheets of graph paper for this activity. On the first sheet, design a "dot-to-dot" picture. Then write the coordinate pairs in the order given, being careful to list the horizontal coordinate first, then the vertical coordinate. Copy your list of coordinate pairs onto a blank sheet of graph paper then give it to a partner to complete. Your design may be simple or elaborate.

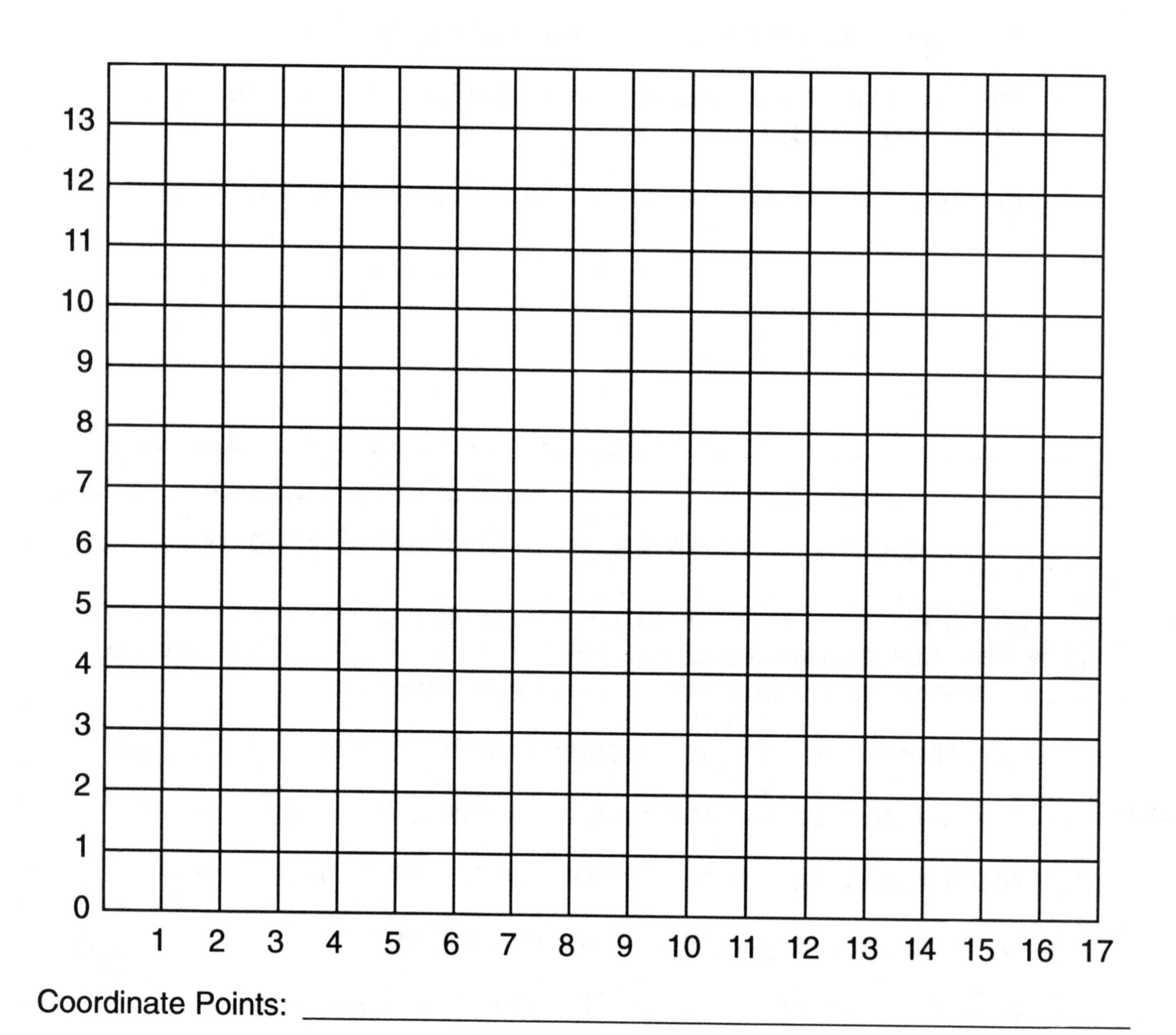

Coordinate Points: ____

____

Designed by: ____________________ Completed by: ____________________

Sample Homework Choices *(cont.)*

Measurement Homework Card #1

Measure each item at your home in the units that are listed. Write your answers below.

Window	**Front door**	**Mirror**	**Refrigerator**
length ____ inches	length ____ inches	length ____ inches	length ____ inches
length____centimeters	length____centimeters	length____centimeters	length____centimeters
width ____ inches	width ____ inches	width ____ inches	width ____ inches
width________centimeters	width________centimeters	width________centimeters	width________centimeters

Measurement Homework Card #2

Ask a parent for permission to do this. Use water, flour, or sugar to find the correct amount for each measurement. If you use water, work by a sink so spills won't be a problem. If you use dry materials, level each spoon or cup with a flat spatula to get an accurate measurement.

How many tablespoons are in one cup?

1 cup = __________ tablespoons

How many tablespoons are in 1/2 cup?

1/2 cup = __________ tablespoons

How many 1/4 cups are in 1 cup?

1 cup = __________ 1/4 cups

How many teaspoons are in 1 tablespoon?

1 tablespoon = __________ teaspoons

How many 1/2 cups are in 3 cups?

3 cups = __________ 1/2 cups

Sample Homework Choices *(cont.)*

Propaganda Homework #1

Propaganda can be defined as presenting an idea to try to influence people's thinking. This assignment can make you think about the ways that advertisements and commercials are designed to influence us.

Read over the examples of propaganda techniques below; then watch TV commercials or read magazine and newspaper advertisements to find examples of five of them. For your answers, you may give a written description, present a video taped segment, or cut ads out of a magazine or newspaper and paste them on a page.

LOADED WORDS:
Use words filled with emotion.
Example: Guaranteed! Best Buy!

SLOGANS:
Simple, catchy phrases used to capture your interest
Example: "Pizza! Pizza!"

BANDWAGON:
Makes you want to go along with the crowd.
Example: The # 1choice of . . .

CARD-STACKING:
They show you only a few of the facts, to favor one side.

NAME-CALLING or MUD-SLINGING:
In politics, to defeat an opponent by smearing his reputation.
Example: "Draft Dodger!"

TESTIMONIAL:
Use a well-known person, athlete, or film star to promote the product.
Example: Tennis shoes promoted by basketball stars.

PLAIN FOLK:
"I'm one of you."
Example: Political candidates

SNOB APPEAL:
Flattery for an elite group
Example: Exclusive products

Propaganda Homework #2:

Weekend TV Assignment

You will need a clock or a watch with a minute hand on it to complete this assignment. Watch 30 minutes of television. Time each commercial you see during that period and write it on the chart. Compute the total minutes of commercials you watched in that half hour. How many minutes were left for the program?

Commercials:	Minutes:
1) ____________________	_______
2) ____________________	_______
3) ____________________	_______
4) ____________________	_______
5) ____________________	_______
6) ____________________	_______

Date: ____________________

Time: ____________________

Show: ____________________

Total minutes of commercials during a ½ hour program. ______________

Amount of time left for the program.

____

Sample Homework Choices *(cont.)*

Grocery Shopping Homework

Name:______________________________ Date Due: ____________

Visit a grocery store. Find the cost without tax for each set of items. You may choose any brand.

Store: __________________________

Set 1—Dairy:

1 dozen eggs __________

1 gallon 2% milk __________

12-ounce package of cheese __________

Total: __________

Set 2—Cereal and Meat:

1—22 oz box of cereal __________

1 pound turkey meat __________

1 pound ground chuck __________

Total: __________

Set 3—Household Items:

4 bars of soap __________

4 rolls of toilet paper __________

1—20 ounce bottle shampoo __________

Total: __________

Set 4—Junk Food:

six ounce potato chips __________

18 oz. package cookies __________

6 pack of soft drinks __________

Total: __________

Set 5—Fruits and Vegetables:

2 lemons __________

1 head of lettuce __________

1 20-ounce can of pineapple __________

Total: __________

Set 6—Condiments:

32 ounce jar of mayonnaise ________

16 ounce bottle of dressing ________

15 ounce bottle of steak sauce ________

Total: ________

What is the total cost of your grocery list? ______________

For an extra challenge, find the tax for taxable items by multiplying the total by ______ %, then add that amount to the cost for your grand total.

Sample Homework Choices *(cont.)*

Book Report Homework

Step 1: Read the book. Select a mystery at an appropriate reading level. You may take up to three weeks to finish the book.

Step 2: Answer the following questions when you finish reading the book.

1. Where does the story take place? ______________________________
2. Who are the main characters in the story? ______________________________
3. What is the mystery that needs to be solved? ______________________________
4. How was the mystery solved? Who solved it? ______________________________
5. List some of the clues that were given to help solve the mystery.

   ____
6. What would you change about the story? ______________________________
7. Name several skills that a detective needs to help him solve a mystery.

   ____
8. Would you like to become a private investigator, policeman, lawyer, or detective?

   ____
9. Give reasons why other students should or should not read this book.

   ____
10. Was there a feeling of suspense during the story? What made it feel that way?

    ____

Step 3: Write your rough draft. Your answers to these questions will help you to write a rough draft of your book report. After completing the rough draft, read it over, making sure that you have an introduction, a body, and a concluding paragraph. Edit carefully for spelling, punctuation, and capitalization errors before writing your final draft.

Step 4: Write your final draft. The final draft will be graded upon the following criteria:

_______ Cover sheet with name, date, and book title

_______ Used pencil, blue ink, black ink, or typed

_______ Handwritten or Typed

_______ Write on every other line

_______ Write on front side of paper only

_______ Mechanics: correct grammar, punctuation, and capitalization

_______ Correct spelling

_______ Introduction: paragraph

_______ Body of report: paragraph(s)

_______ Conclusion: paragraph

Assessment

Parent and Child Goal Sheet

Please fill out the goal sheet with your child, including information about your child's needs, interests, and abilities.

ACADEMIC

1. What are your child's strongest academic areas? ______________________________

   ____

2. Name some special interests of your child. ______________________________

   ____

3. What three goals should the child begin the year with? ______________________

   ____

4. In what academic area does your child need additional work? ________________

   ____

SOCIAL

1. What are the child's strongest social skills? ______________________________

   ____

2. What would be an appropriate social goal for your child? ____________________

   ____

PHYSICAL

1. What are the child's strongest physical abilities and interests? ______________

   ____

2. What does the child need additional work on physically? ____________________

   ____

EMOTIONAL

1. Name things that make your child very happy: ______________________________

   angry: ____

   sad: ____

2. Does the child have a fear of anything which would relate to school? If so, what?

   ____

Please make any additional comments which you feel are appropriate. ______________

____

____

Student Signature ______________________________

Parent Signature ______________________________ Date: ____________

Adapted from Elizabeth Lolli, Multi-Age Classrooms: *The Ungrading of America's Schools*, 1993.

Sample STP (Student, Teacher, and Parent) Goals

Scheduling a Student, Teacher, and Parent conference at the beginning of the school year presents an excellent opportunity to set at least three appropriate goals for the student. As goals are accomplished or progress is made, additional goals may be established. If a goal is found to be inappropriate, it may be changed. Goals may relate to work habits and independent studies, rather than merely relating to academics. A general target date for achieving these goals should be agreed upon by all parties.

Suggested Goals

Academics

- Choose challenging books to read from the library.
- Learn how to multiply 2-digit x 2-digit numbers.
- Improve on speed and accuracy of basic math facts.
- Learn cursive handwriting and write a story in cursive.
- Write complete sentences using capitals and punctuation appropriately.
- Learn how to tell time and count money.
- Memorize addition, subtraction, and multiplication facts.
- Learn to calculate and apply division concepts.
- Improve in spelling words correctly. Focus on vowel patterns and word parts.
- Combine related sentences into paragraphs.

Work Habits

- Join groups appropriately by paying attention and not disturbing others.
- Organize what needs to be taken home before being dismissed daily.
- Complete the Beginning School Assignments daily.
- Be responsible about personal needs such as lunch money and homework.
- Feel confident in asking questions and in asking for help with assignments.
- Improve on following directions, completing assignments, and joining the group appropriately.
- Keep papers in appropriate folders and keep your desk area organized and clean.
- Be responsible for completing centers and sharing a center project with a group.

Independent Studies

- Finish typing "Reach for the Stars" essay and submit it for the competition.
- Outline independent study plans that relate to units being studied. Take planning sheet home; get it signed, and return it to school.
- Finish, print, and publish a copy of the Storybook Weaver story.
- Teach a group of students how to finger weave.
- Learn how to operate the video editing machine, and teach others how to use the editor.
- Complete an independent research study on Koalas and use technology to create the final product.
- Write and publish a story about the Civil War era from the viewpoint of a slave.
- Research and conduct experiments about bacteria and parasites.

Portfolio Assessment

Portfolios

Portfolios are a purposeful collection of student work to show evidence of a child's learning, efforts, progress and achievement in one or more areas. They show the big picture of a student's growth over time, not just a snapshot. Portfolios are a wonderful tool for assessing a student's ability to produce, perceive, and reflect. Students are responsible for making contributions and updating their portfolio with quality work. Also, portfolios provide concrete items for students to share during parent conferences. Students benefit by feeling a sense of ownership, responsibility, and pride in themselves and their learning.

Menu of a Portfolio

Table of Contents
Letter From the Student to the Reader of the Portfolio Explaining Contents
Interest Inventory
Parent and Child Goal Sheet
Continuous List of Goals and Progress
Self Portrait
Self-Evaluation Forms
Peer Evaluation Forms
Teacher Checklists / Anecdotal Records
Attitude Surveys (for various school subjects)
Writing Samples—Rough Draft (Sloppy Copy), Editing Checklist, Final Draft (Neat Sheet)
Spelling Samples—(Fall, Winter, and Spring)
Papers That Show the Student's Correction of Errors and Misconceptions
Reading Log
Reading Response Journal
Audio / Video Tapes of Reading
Math and Science Journals (with manipulatives)
Photographs and Samples of Projects
Collaborative Project Samples
Independent Study Projects and Samples
Art Work
Videotapes
Computer Disks
Evidence of Technology Use
Evidence of Achievements Outside of School
Comments Page

Student-led Conferencing Preparation Sheet

This sheet can be given to children before they share their portfolios. Responses to these statements help guide students when sharing their portfolios.

My Accomplishments

Name: ______________________________ Date: ______________

1. Two things I've done well this year are ______________________

   ____

2. The most important thing that I am trying to do in our classroom is ______

   ____

3. Something that I am proud about this year is ______________________

   ____

4. One thing I think I need to work harder on is______________________

   ____

5. If I could change or redo one of my projects, I would ______________

   ____

6. The hardest thing that I have had to figure out or learn about this year is

   ____

7. I have accomplished the following goals ______________________

   ____

8. A new goal that I want to achieve is______________________

   ____

Portfolio Prompts for Sharing Opportunities

These prompts can be displayed on a classroom chart to help give parents and visitors an idea of what to say to students as they share their portfolios. Also, teachers may create a page of questions that can be asked about a particular piece in the portfolio to provide more insight into the process or of the child's understanding of the subject area.

1. Tell me about this project or activity.
2. What did you try? What steps did you take?
3. What was difficult or did not work?
4. How do you feel about the piece?
5. What would you like to change about this piece?
6. What does this show that you have learned?
7. Tell me what you learned.
8. Why did you choose this piece for your portfolio?
9. What is your favorite piece? Why?
10. What was the easiest or most difficult part of the activity?
11. What are your strengths?
12. What are your weaknesses?
13. I was surprised that ____.
14. I noticed that ____.
15. I was pleased that ____.
16. What does ____ mean?

Assessment Questioning

Teachers can use these questions during conferences to encourage students to thoughtfully refect upon their learning. In addition, the questions can be used for instructional purposes to stimulate ideas for further investigation. The questions focus on students understanding, explaining, trying a variety of strategies, analyzing processes and solutions, and being able to transfer and apply knowledge. Remember to give students plenty of time to give thoughtful answers.

- What is this problem about? What are you being asked?
- Please explain that in your own words.
- Do you have all the information that you need?
- What else would you like to know?
- What assumptions did you have to make?
- Where can you find the information that you need?
- What have you already tried? What worked?
- What seemed to be the problem?
- Have you tried drawing an illustration or diagram to help you?
- Do you see a pattern?
- Let's break this down into parts. What is the first thing that you need to do?
- Did you make a prediction or estimate?
- Is there another way that you could do that?
- How would you explain that to a younger child?
- Have you discussed that idea with your group? What do they think?
- Are there other possible solutions?
- Is there anything that you have overlooked or forgotten?
- Is that a reasonable answer?
- What made you think that was what you were supposed to do?
- Have you thought of any new questions now?
- How would the situation change if ______________________________?
- Does this make you think of anything else that you have done before?
- Is there anything that you would do differently next time?
- Evaluate your own progress. How did things go? How do you think you did?

This form is to be completed by all students working in cooperative groups. By setting their own goals and evaluating their efforts, students acquire more responsibility and ownership in the group's progress. Keeping this form available during the work process helps the group keep their goals in mind.

Group Planning and Evaluation Sheet

Planning

Fill out this form with your teammates.

Activity: ______________________________ Beginning Date: ____________

Group Members: ____

____

What We Are Going to Do: ______________________________________

____

____

Materials We Need: ____

____

____

Evaluation

Score your team together. Circle the appropriate rating.

1. Completing the assignment
   Needs Improvement *Good* *Excellent*
2. Reading and following directions carefully
   Needs Improvement *Good* *Excellent*
3. Being responsible to keep up with our materials
   Needs Improvement *Good* *Excellent*
4. Cooperating with each other
   Needs Improvement *Good* *Excellent*
5. Everyone is participating equally
   Needs Improvement *Good* *Excellent*

Sample Student Report Card

INTERMEDIATE MULTI-AGE

LANGUAGE ARTS AND MATHEMATICS will be marked using letter grades: A B C or I

SOCIAL STUDIES, SCIENCE, HANDWRITING, HEALTH/SAFETY, ART, MUSIC, AND PHYSICAL EDUCATION will be marked: S = Satisfactory N = Needs Improvement I = Incomplete

The remaining areas concerning STUDY HABITS AND SOCIAL/EMOTIONAL GROWTH will be marked:

AL = Always O = Often T = Some Times R = Rarely

Student Name Robert Williams

Grade Multi-Age - 3rd

Teacher Marsha Bond

SUBJECT		REPORTING PERIOD						
		1	2	3	4	5	6	Final
Language Arts		B						
Math		B						
Social Studies		S						
Science		S						
Handwriting		St						
Health/Safety		S						
Art		S						
Music		S						
Physical Education		S						
Works/Plays Well with Others		T						
Completes Tasks on Time		O						
Maintains Self-Control		T						
Has Positive Self-Esteem		O						
Shows Proper Respect		O						
Listens Appropriately		T						
Effort Equal to Ability		O						
ATTENDANCE	Tardy	O						
	Absent	I						

STP GOALS (Student/Teacher/Parent)
PROGRESS MADE/ACCOMPLISHED/SET NEW GOALS

1. Read one book each week. – Accomplished!
2. Learn how to spell words correctly and retain previous spelling words. – Progress made!
3. Understand subtraction with regrouping. – Some progress.

STP Comments

The following comment section is set up to be used by all parties (STP) at the completion of a nine week period. The teachers will be commenting when appropriate on the following topics concerning your child's growth and development:

1. Assuming responsibility for actions and learning.
2. Contributing to the classroom and school.
3. Being a complex thinker.
4. Working collaboratively.

We encourage you to make positive and constructive comments.

STP COMMENTS (cont.)

Robert is a neat writer and enjoys sharing his ideas! He has already printed a story on the computer using the program "My Own Story."

Robert sounds out word parts when he reads. This causes him to read slowly. He reads below grade level but comprehends what he reads.

In math he needs to keep practicing the basic math facts.

He needs to exercise self control when on the playground.

This report card is designed to encourage constructive remarks and responses from students, parents, and teachers. The child's goals are listed in the STP Goals section and are updated continuously. This report card can be used for six-week as well as nine-week reports. It includes information about the child's academics, study habits, and social/emotional growth.

Answer Key

Page 90

Math Computation Skills Assessment

1. eight thousand, three hundred seventy-six
2. 5,000 + 400 + 8
3. I=1, C=100, X=10, V=5
4. 0, 2, 4, 6, 8, 10, 12,
   4, 8, 12, 16, 20, 24,
   5, 10, 15, 20, 25, 30, 35
   27, 30, 33, 36, 39, 42, 45
   88, 80, 72, 64, 56, 48, 40
   32, 37, 42, 47, 52, 57
   0, 1/4, 2/4, 3/4, 4/4, 5/4, 6/4
   6.50, 6.75, 7.00, 7.25, 7.50, 7.75, 8.00
5. $.61
6. $.84
7. 498
8. 825
9. 1,161
10. 142
11. 27
12. 37
13. 50
14. 95
15. 149,132
16. $147.54
17. 668
18. 143
19. 26
20. 27,399
21. $3.04
22. 28
23. 63
24. $5\frac{1}{2}$
25. $2\frac{3}{4}$
26. 740
27. 2,666
28. 14,476
29. 20,720
30. 5
31. 4R2
32. 15

Page 91 Multiplication Facts Sheet

1. 0, 24, 35, 42, 45, 4, 6, 8, 6, 0
2. 0, 21, 30, 35, 36, 3, 4, 4, 0, 72
3. 0, 12, 15, 14, 9, 0, 18, 32, 42, 48
4. 0, 6, 5, 0, 81, 8, 14, 24, 30, 32
5. 0, 0, 45, 56, 63, 6, 10, 16, 18, 16
6. 0, 27, 40, 49, 54, 5, 8, 12, 12, 8
7. 0, 9, 10, 7, 0, 9, 16, 28, 36, 40
8. 0, 3, 0, 63, 72, 7, 12, 20, 24, 24
9. 0, 15, 20, 21, 18, 1, 0, 36, 48, 56
10. 0, 18, 25, 28, 27, 2, 2, 0, 54, 64

Page 92—Ladder Math I

1. 59
2. 101
3. 133
4. 1,610
5. 41
6. 16
7. 32
8. 188
9. 2,868
10. 20
11. 56
12. 80
13. 64
14. 1,923
15. 623
16. 2,634
17. 2,226
18. 630
19. 29,580
20. 3
21. 9
22. 6r1 or 6 1/3
23. 8r5 or 8 5/7
24. 85r2 or 85 2/5
25. 8r6 or 8 3/5
26. 293r4 or 293 $\frac{1}{3}$
27. 1,537r8

Page 93 Ladder Math II

1. 96
2. 47
3. 688
4. 944
5. 653
6. 114
7. 12,404
8. $4.44
9. 15
10. 35
11. 47
12. 57
13. 16
14. 296
15. 467
16. 288
17. 178
18. $1.98
19. 929
20. 4,319
21. 42
22. 304
23. 520
24. 4,200
25. $55.20
26. 2,241
27. 2,844
28. 4,500
29. 25,296
30. 596,000
31. 279,832
32. 52r1 or $52\frac{1}{3}$
33. 1,895r3 or $1{,}895\frac{3}{5}$
34. 787

Answer Key *(cont.)*

Page 94—Mid-Year Math Assessment

1. 6, 8, 10, 12, 14, 16, 18
2. 15, 18, 21, 24, 27, 30, 33
3. 90, 80, 70, 60, 50, 40,
4. 60, 55, 50, 45, 40, 35, 30
5. 4, 8, 12, 16, 20, 24, 28
6. 36, 33, 30, 27, 24, 21, 18
7. eight hundred forty-nine
8. one thousand two hundred ten
9. thirty-six
10. 700 + 20 + 5
11. 3,000 + 600 + 90 + 1
12. 200 + 4
13. 30
14. 70
15. 100
16. $.72
17. 579
18. 806
19. 42
20. 17
21. 133
22. 817
23. 24
24. 60
25. 28
26. 3
27. 3
28. 6
29. >
30. <
31. <
32. =
33. <
34. =

Page 95—Challenging Mid-Year Math Assessment

1. six hundred ninety thousand, four hundred fifty-eight
   600,000 + 90,000 + 400 + 50 + 8
2. twelve thousand, seven hundred three
   10,000 + 2,000 + 700 + 3
3. LXVII
4. CL
5. XXIX
6. first, second, third, fourth, fifth, sixth, seventh, eighth,
   ninth, tenth, eleventh
7. 400
8. 1,700
9. twelve hundredths
10. thirty-nine and five hundredths
11. 5,824
12. $376.64
13. 123,035
14. 109.55
15. 1,088
16. $132.48
17. 6,384
18. 101
19. 5R8
20. $1.39
21. 24.83
22. 3,389
23. 9 weeks
24. 130 minutes
25. 4
26. 3/4 or .75
27. 3
28. >
29. <
30. >
31. <
32. >
33. >
34. <
35. >
36. =
37. >
38. =

29. **Page 106 *Number the Stars*—Grolier Hunt Answers**

1. North Sea and Baltic Sea
2. Copenhagen
3. Six million
4. Poland
5. Roosevelt
6. South
7. Germany
8. "one giant leap for mankind"
9. Soviet Union
12. roll, yaw, pitch

Page 107 Revolution—Grolier Hunt Answers

1. Ticonderoga
2. commander
3. the north
4. Treaty of Paris
5. George Washington's
6. Thomas Jefferson
7. Alexander Hamilton
8. militia, Lexington
9. Connecticut, Rhode Island, New York, Vermont, New Hampshire
10. peace, harmony

Matrix Puzzles—page 112

1. Crumley is the comic writer, Adams is the nurse, and Wood is the engineer.
2. Chris is the computer programmer, Alan is the artist, Emily is the sales person, and Jacquelyn is the chief executive.

Matrix Puzzles—page 113

3. Carlin ate popcorn, David ate ice cream, Ashley ate bacon, and Shanna ate carrots.
4. April won the helium balloon, Krystal won the stuffed animal, Paul won the glove, Scott won the playdough, and Tyler won the hat.

Answer Key *(cont.)*

Page 119 Body Systems

1. 200
2. Lungs
3. Circulatory system
4. Potatoes, rice, and bread
5. Epiglottis
6. White blood cells, red blood cells, plasma, platelets, or hemoglobin
7. Vertebrae
8. Platelets
9. To the large intestine
10. Diaphram
11. White blood cells
12. Esophagus
13. Respiratory
14. Arteries
15. The skull
16. Alveoli
17. The digestive system
18. The skull
19. Carbon dioxide
20. Phalanges
21. Knees and elbows—Allow bones to move in two directions.
22. Veins
23. Oxygen
24. Humerus, ulna, radius
25. Larynx
26. Kidney
27. Calcium
28. Ligaments
29. Ball and socket, hinge, pivot, and gliding joints

Page 123 Revolution Homework

Card 1

1. executives
2. patriots
3. delegates
4. oaths
5. amendments
6. sentries
7. territories
8. colonies
9. speeches
10. children
11. assemblies
12. cities
13. minutemen
14. branches

Card 2

1. Virginia's and Georgia's delegates
2. Paul Revere's jobs
3. John Hancock's signature
4. Sam Adam's loyal dog
5. John Hancock's fancy clothes
6. Patrick Henry's speech
7. Southern Colonies' plantations
8. Washington's army

Page 124 Revolution Homework

Card 3

1. warned
2. rode
3. wrote
4. voted
5. noticed
6. gave
7. approved
8. revised
9. convinced
10. rang
11. married
12. threw

Card 4

1. mús-ket
2. de-clar-á-tion
3. in-de-pen´-dence
4. Con´-cord
5. Lex´-ing-ton
6. Phil-a-dél-phi-a
7. pá-tri-ot
8. In´-di-an
9. Loy´-al-ist
10. cam´-o-flage
11. nap´-sack
12. per-sis´-tent
13. traí-tor
14. bay-o-nét
15. tri-um´-phant

Page 125 Revolution Homework

Card 5

1. The Boston Tea Party happened on December 16, 1773.
2. The First Continental Congress met on October 26, 1774.
3. The United States and Great Britain signed the Treaty of Paris on September 3, 1783.
4. The Declaration of Independence was adopted on July 4, 1776.

Card 6

1. Sam refused to ride a horse, but John convinced him to try.
2. Men dressed like Indians, and they threw tea off the ship.
3. Ben invented many things, and we remember him today.
4. Men disagreed with the taxes, so they refused to pay them.
5. King George acted like he wasn't worried about the war, yet he didn't know how to make the people in America behave.

Bibliography

American Association of School Administrators. *The Nongraded Primary: Making Schools Fit Children,* Arlington, VA, 1992.

Anderson, Robert H., and Barbara Nelson Pavan. *Nongradedness: Helping It to Happen.* Lancaster, PA: Technomic Press, 1992.

Armstrong, Thomas. *In Their Own Way, Discovering and Encouraging Your Child's Personal Learning Style.* Los Angeles: J.P. Tarcher, 1987.

Baratta-Lorton, Robert. *Mathematics...A Way Of Thinking.* Reading, MS: Addison-Wesley Publishing Company, 1977.

Butzow, Carol M., and John W. Butzow. *Science Through Children's Literature: An Integrated Approach.* Englewood, Colorado: Teacher Ideas Press, 1989.

Chase, Penelle, and Joan Doan. *Full Circle: A New Look at Multi-Age Education.* Portsmouth, NH: Heinemann, 1994.

Cook, Carole. *Math Learning Centers for the Primary Grades.* West Nynack, NY: The Center for Applied Research, 1992.

Council of State Governments. *State Administrative Officials.* Lexington, KY: Council of State Governmments, 1992.

Curran, Lorna. *Cooperative Learning Lessons for Little Ones: Literature-Based Language Arts and Social Skills.* San Juan Capistrano, CA: Resources for Teachers, Inc., 1992.

Ellis, Susan S., and Susan F. Whalen. *Cooperative Learning: Getting Started.* New York: Scholastic, 1990.

Fogarty, Robin. *The Mindful School: How to Integrate the Curricula.* Palatine, IL: Skylight Publishing, Inc., 1991.

Gardner, Howard. *Frames of Mind: The Theory of Multiple Intelligences.* New York: Basic Books, 1985.

Gardner, Howard. *The Unschooled Mind: How Children Think and How Schools Should Teach.* New York: Basic Books, 1991.

Gayfer, Margaret, Ed. *The Multi-grade Classroom: Myth and Reality.* Toronto: Canadian Education Association, 1991.

Goodlad, John I., and Robert H. Anderson, *The Nongraded Elementary School.* New York: Teachers College Press, 1987.

Goodman, Kenneth S., Lois Bridges Bird, and Yetta Goodman. *The Whole Language Catalogue.* Santa Rosa, CA: American School Publishers, 1991.

Grant, Jim. *Development Education in the 1990s.* Rosemont, NJ: Modern Learning Press, 1991.

Grant, Jim. *I Hate School! Some Commonsense Answers for Parents Who Wonder Why.* Rosemont, NJ: Programs for Education, 1986.

Grant, Jim. *Worth Repeating: Giving Children a Second Chance at School Success.* Rosemont, NJ: Modern Learning Press/Programs for Education, 1989.

Grant, Jim, and Robert. A Johnson, *Common Sense Guide to Multi-Age Practices.* Columbus, OH: Teacher's Publishing Group, 1994.

Bibliography *(cont.)*

Hodges, John C., and Mary Whitten. *Harbrace College Handbook, Tenth Edition.* Chicago, IL: Harcourt Brace Jovanovich, 1986.

Hoskisson, Kenneth, and Gail E Tompkins. *Language Arts: Content and Teaching Strategies.* New York, NY: Macmillan Publishing Company, 1991.

Hunter, Madeline. *How to Change to a Nongraded School.* Alexandria, VA: Association for Supervision and Curriculum Development, 1992.

Kasten, Wendy, and Barbara Clarke,. *The Multi-Age Classroom.* Katonah, NY: Richard C. Owen, 1993.

Katz, Lilian G., and Silvia C. Chard. *Engaging Children's Minds: The Project Approach.* Norwood, NJ: Ablex, 1990.

Katz, Lilian G., Demetra Evangelou, and Jeanette Hartman. *The Case for Mixed-Age Grouping in Early Education.* Washington, DC: (NAEYC) National Association for the Education of Young Children, 1990.

Kohn, Alfie. *No Contest: The Case Against Competition.* Boston: Houghton Mifflin Company, 1986.

Lingelbach, Jenepher. *Hands-On Nature: Exploring the Environment.* Woodstock, VT: Vermont Institute of Natural Science, 1986.

Maeda, Bev. *The Multi-Age Classroom.* Cypress, CA: Creative Teaching Press, 1994.

Manitoba Department of Education. *Language Arts Handbook for Primary Teachers in Multigrade Classrooms.* Winnipeg, Manitoba, 1988.

Miller, Bruce A. *The Multigrade Classroom: A Resource Handbook for Small Rural Schools.* Portland, OR: Northwest Regional Educational Laboratory, 1989.

Rathborne, Charles, Anne Bingham, Peggy Dorta, Molley McClaskey, and Justine O'Keefe. *Multi-Age Portraits: Teaching and Learning in Mixed-age Classrooms.* Peterborough, NH: Crystal Springs Books, 1993.

Society For Development Education. *Into Teacher's Hands* (5th Ed. SDE Sourcebook). Peterborough, NH: 1992.

Society For Development Education. *Multi-Age Classrooms: The Ungrading of America's Schools.* Peterborough, NH: 1993.

Virginia Education Association and Appalachia Educational Laboratory. *Teaching Combined Grade Classes: Real Problems and Promising Practices.* Charleston, WV: AEL, 1990.

Parts of a Book Center—book sources

Beyer, Barry. *United States and Its Neighbors: The World Around Us.* New York, NY: Macmillan Publishing Co., 1990.

Orfan, Lucy J. and Bruce R. Vogeli. *Mathematics, Grade 4.* Atlanta, GA: Silver Burdett Company, 1987.

Pearson, P. David. *Silver Secrets.* Atlanta, GA: Silver Burdett and Ginn, Inc., 1989.

Sund, Dr. Robert, Dr. Donald Adams, and Dr. Jay Hackett. *Accent on Science.* Columbus, Ohio: Charles E. Merrill Publishing Company, 1980.